A GUIDE TO
MAJOR HOUSE
REPAIRS

A GUIDE TO MAJOR HOUSE REPAIRS

Geoffrey West

THE CROWOOD PRESS

First published in 2012 by
The Crowood Press Ltd
Ramsbury, Marlborough
Wiltshire SN8 2HR

www.crowood.com

British Library Cataloguing-in-Publication Data
A catalogue record for this book is available from the British Library.

ISBN 978 1 84797 386 3

Disclaimer
All tools and equipment used in connection with house repair should be operated in strict
accordance with both the current health and safety regulations and the manufacturer's
instructions. The author and publisher do not accept any responsibility or liability of any
kind in any manner whatsoever for any error or omission, or any loss, damage, injury or
adverse outcome incurred as result of the use of any of the information contained in this
book, or reliance upon it. If in doubt about any aspect of architectural salvage readers are
advised to seek professional advice. The fact that particular tradespeople are mentioned in
this publication does not indicate that either the publishers, or the author, are necessarily
recommending them in preference to any others who are not mentioned herein.

Typeset by Jean Cussons Typesetting, Diss, Norfolk
Printed and bound in Malaysia by Times Offset (M) Sdn Bhd

Contents

Acknowledgements

I am indebted to Brian Clancy (structural engineer) who thoroughly and tirelessly checked the subsidence section, correcting errors and giving me some marvellous pictures that I couldn't have got from anywhere else. Steve Hodgson, general manager of the Property Care Association (PCA) and Sue Uttridge, also of the PCA, patiently checked my facts about cavity wall-tie matters, and found me some excellent pictures. I'd also like to thank Laura Mason of the National Federation of Roofing Contractors, who went to endless trouble finding me pictures, as did Technical Manager Bill Jenkins, who corrected my copy in the flat-roof section.

I'd also like to thank Jayne Runacres and Brian Berry, Director of External Affairs at the Federation of Master Builders (FMB), who went to a great deal of effort correcting and altering the section on finding a builder, giving me pictures and adding crucial facts that I had left out. Thanks also to: Julian Owen, for letting me use his comments and also supplying me with plenty of pictures; Roy Ilott for his support over the years and help with some excellent pictures; Beverley Winterhalter for her quote regarding getting finance and mortgages; Robert Hooker for his comments regarding insurance. Ken Warren, expert in damp problems, as always gave me a succinct and useful quote, as did John Dee, regarding cavity wall-tie failure and Brian Ridout gave me some fine pictures.

Additionally, Bethany Winning of the Royal Institute of British Architects (RIBA) corrected me on several points and gave me helpful information, as did Shona Broughton of the Association of Consultant Architects (ACA). Allister Moorcroft, of H. Docherty Ltd, gave me useful information on HETAS, and let me use text from his website, and Michael Carr of the National Association of Chimney Engineers (NACE) helped too. Joanna Haydon Knowell helped with facts concerning estate agency. Final thanks to: Roger Mears; Hayley Mountstevens of ZPR public relations (who helped regarding permission for taking pictures at B&Q); Sharon Hutchings of the Institute of Carpenters (IOC); Neal Hollenberry of Floodtite Systems ltd, who gave me some fine images. Roger Willis also gave me plenty of assistance.

The above experts and officials have helped and corrected some parts of the following, but I'd like to stress that any mistakes are my own, and should not be connected with any of the above people.

And love and thanks to Olga for her help and support.

Introduction

This is not a DIY book or an instructional building manual. It's a guide that tells you, in straightforward terms, what is meant by various building catastrophes, so that when you're employing people to help you sort things out, you can understand what they're talking about and grasp the basic principles of what's to be done. For British readers, it also outlines the various trade federations whom you can approach when trying to find the right person to do a particular job. All these organizations/federations have websites and lists of their members according to area. Some are more helpful than others, and I have particularly mentioned the agreeable ones who had the courtesy and kindness to find time to help me.

Houses are reasonably straightforward structures and there are universal problems, many of which are caused by the effects of weathering, especially the ingress of water, a great deal by bungling builders or DIYers, who can often do far more harm than good, and occasionally by factors no one has any control over, such as freak weather or subsidence, or of course wilful damage.

The majority of house disasters are the effects of neglect over a long period of time. Consider a derelict uninhabited cottage. The roof is damaged, allowing water into the structure and, therefore, rot develops in the timbers, allowing plasters and other materials to degrade and collapse. If one person lives in a house for many years, they may get used to problems so that they eventually hardly notice them, and these faults can creep up almost unnoticed until drastic damage is done. But for every major catastrophe, there are many smaller problems that can be fixed quite easily.

One obvious fact about very old houses is that if they are still in existence they must have been basically sound to start with. A great many 'speculative' builders constructed houses in the Victorian boom time, and some of these collapsed shortly afterwards. This was in the days before building regulations: a typical fault that could prove terminal was shallow foundations, which were sometimes too insubstantial to support the building's weight. Since that time, building regulations have been introduced to force correct practices in construction and ensure that more recently built houses are unlikely to have inherent defects. However, even ancient timber-framed houses that slope alarmingly sideways can be structurally perfectly sound. Medieval timber that is peppered with woodworm holes can often be tremendously strong, because the pest typically only eats the outer inch or so of this kind of rock-hard ancient oak timber, leaving the solid heartwood undamaged and as strong as it was half a century ago. The earliest timber-framed houses were built by shipwrights, who initially based the 'skeleton' of the house on that of a ship's frame. The fundamentals of structural engineering were not understood at first, meaning that these early houses were built with the floor joists laid flat instead of on edge, as they are today, meaning that floors were apt to be 'springy' and unsupportive. This, in turn, necessitated an overhang of the upper storey over the lower, as a rudimentary method of spreading the weight, creating what was known as a 'jetty'. This jetty also had the advantage of allowing foul water thrown from upper storey windows to reach the outside edge of the pavement rather than the inner side, possibly the reason why a gentleman traditionally walked on the roadside edge of the pavement, shielding a lady, who would normally walk on the inner, building, side.

There are particular problems when you are repairing a building that is 'listed', because you have to get each stage of the work approved by the conservation officer who works for your local authority. He or she is likely to stipulate particular materials and methods of working, which may be more costly than standard procedures. However, these officers have an affinity with old buildings, and if you are in a position to rescue one from dilapidation, they are likely to be on your side and will make efforts to compromise as much as they can.

Whether you have discovered a problem with your own property, are considering purchasing a building with defects or are just curious about what 'kills' a building, and the manner of specialist care that is needed, this book should lift the lid on building dilemmas of all kinds and tell you how to get them solved. There is nothing as rewarding and satisfying as curing a building of its fundamental problems, and if you superintend the work yourself, and are able locate the right professionals, you can ultimately save money, as well as bringing your building back to health and adding to its value.

If you come across a term you're not familiar with, look at the end of the book in the Glossary.

CHAPTER 1

Understanding the Survey

THE SURVEY

If you are looking at a property to buy, your lender will insist on a valuation, which is the simplest and cheapest assessment, principally just to make sure the house is worth more than their loan to you in a forced-sale situation. The 'Homebuyer Survey and Valuation' (HSV), also known as a Homebuyer's Report, is a survey completed to a standard format set out by the Royal Institution of Chartered Surveyors (RICS), and is most suitable for conventional properties built within the last 150 years, that are in reasonable condition. The equivalent of what was once referred to as the 'Full Structural Survey' is now called the 'Building Survey', and is the most detailed of all, being a comprehensive inspection of a property reported in a style to suit the property and your specific requirements; it examines all accessible parts of the property, and is suitable for all types of building, particularly older and/or listed properties, buildings of any age

A major partial house collapse, with the chimney-breast supported by a steel joist.

Closer view of the chimney-breast support, with timbers supporting the brickwork.

constructed in an unusual way, properties you plan to alter or renovate or those that have had radical alterations.

The Homebuyer Survey and Valuation (HSV)

Not every aspect of the property is detailed and this report focuses only on urgent matters requiring attention; generally it is not suitable for properties in need of renovation, or buildings for which you are planning drastic alterations. Basically, the HSV gives you details about the general condition of the property, any major faults in accessible parts of the building that can affect its value, urgent problems that need inspecting by a specialist, the result of a test for damp in walls, if there is damage to timbers (including rot and woodworm), the condition of any damp-proofing, insulation and drainage (not including a drain test), the estimated cost of rebuilding the property for insurance purposes and the value of the property.

The Building Survey

A thoroughly comprehensive inspection of a property reported in a style to suit it and your own specific requirements. This is suitable for all properties, particularly listed buildings and older properties, buildings that you plan to alter or renovate in any way, constructions that are built in an unusual manner (irrespective of their age), buildings you plan to renovate or alter, as well as those that have had extensive alterations.

The Building Survey examines all accessible parts of the building, and you can request for specific areas to be included, so that it covers any particular concerns you have about the building. It is a service that can be adapted to your specific needs, on agreement with your surveyor. It can include details of minor and major defects and their implications, the possible cost of repairs, the results of damp-testing on walls, whether there is damage to timbers (for instance woodworm/rot), the condition of the damp-proofing, insulation and drainage

An outside wastewater gulley with pipes held in place by string.

(not including a drain test), technical information regarding the construction of the property and the materials used. In addition, there should also be included details of the location and recommendations for any required further special inspections. It does not include a valuation – ask for this separately if you need one.

General Aspects of the Survey

Even in the comprehensive Building Survey, the surveyor cannot lift carpets (fitted or otherwise) or move furniture, because of the possibility of costly damage occurring. Because a surveyor can be held legally accountable for their report, it has to be couched in defensive terms, so that if, for instance, the electrical wiring or plumbing pipework appears at fault, there will be recommendations for a specialist electrical contractor or plumber to make further investigations, because only a relevantly qualified specialist can make a valid assessment.

Some people argue that a good builder is likely to spot the same kinds of problem that a surveyor will highlight; bear in mind, however, that a surveyor is legally bound by his findings and a builder is not. If you are examining a property yourself, there's nothing to stop you asking the current owner if you can lift a carpet, even raise a floorboard, to

check for dry rot or woodworm if this is suspected, but the risk is yours if damage occurs, and you will have to make reparation. A surveyor cannot get into this kind of situation.

The surveyor has a set number of aspects of the building to check and, because his personal insurance liability is a factor, he'll be understandably wary of putting things in writing that aren't covered in get-out phrases. One option, if you're looking at different or older houses that have problems, is to have a thorough preliminary examination yourself, thereby weeding out those with major

Stainless steel manhole cover, much lighter than cast-iron covers.

problems, and only spending money on a Building Survey (if you want more than your lender's HSV survey) on something you are seriously considering for purchase. What's more, if you've already carefully examined a property, you can talk to your surveyor beforehand and draw his or her attention to anything you may have noticed, so they can look carefully at this potential fault.

A survey ordered by your building society is something that can cause concern, because anything discovered is reported to them, and they may hold back part of the loan until the problem has been attended to, which paradoxically reduces your money at precisely the time you need more. However, a survey ordered by you personally serves not only to help you know what you're taking on, but can also be a valuable tool to negotiate a price reduction with the vendor, which is something you may be forced to do anyway if your building society withholds part of their loan offer. It is claimed that the cost of a Building Survey can often at least be covered by the discovery of just one price-reducing fault.

UNDERSTANDING A BUILDING SURVEY REPORT

A surveyor's Building Survey will follow his/her own format, but as a guide, there follows how one leading surveyor presents his findings. Your own Building Survey may not be in this style and may have more or less detail, and additional sections may be added where needed. However, the general content of information presented here shows the kind of report you can expect.

General Information

Introduction

A summary of what the surveyor has been asked to do and the property's circumstances; for example, whether it is presently occupied and is in general decorative order. It normally states 'inspection of structural elements, testing of perimeter walls for rising damp, roof inspected from ground level'. Limitations of the examination are itemized, typically: fitted carpets cannot normally be raised, furniture is not moved, manhole covers (to examine condition of main drains) are not lifted and parts of the building occupied by other people (for instance when considering a flat within a building) are not viewed.

Description

States the general type of building, e.g. bungalow, flat, semi-detached house; the main layout, what the walls and floors are made of, whether it's a Listed Building or is within a Conservation Area (see Chapter 3); also, a comment on the property's age, any extensions or additions that appear to be recently added and the type of site.

Situation

Meaning the building in relation to other properties; for instance, whether it is in a row of similar buildings or a flat within a larger residence; whether it has outbuildings, parking facilities and access to roads; comments on the condition of boundaries (walls or fences) and, if possible, details of any rights of way.

Accommodation

Each room is described, including kitchen and bathroom fittings. Sometimes measurements may be given.

Structure

External Walls

Type of construction, e.g. solid brick or brick with cavity or stone; external finish, if any, and its general condition. Presence of any cracks, sometimes with an opinion as to their cause; any obvious visible problems, e.g. defective pointing, damp or salt-staining.

Internal Walls

Stating what the likely material of the partition walls is, with the proviso that plaster cannot be removed to confirm this assessment.

Windows and Doors

What these are made of (e.g. timber, PVCU), their serviceability, whether window putty needs replacing, the condition of protective paintwork.

Roofs

The type of roof, whether it is tiled, slated, felted

ABOVE: **Cracked stone or concrete windowsill and rotting timber windows.**

BELOW: **Rotting timber windowsill, where protective paint has peeled away.**

This chimney looks as if it needs repointing. Note the gaps between bricks.

or covered with lead. The apparent state of repair, usually as judged from ground level.

Chimney-Stacks/Chimneys
Assessed from the ground level.

Ceilings
Whether these are original, what they are made of, if they incorporate soundproofing materials and their condition. Nowadays 'lath and plaster' ceilings are sometimes criticized in surveyors' reports; however, if they are in good condition, these ceilings are perfectly acceptable.

Floors
The construction material for the floor in each room, their general state, if there's any evidence of fungal or woodworm attack. Be aware that fitted carpets preclude such investigations and floorboards cannot normally be raised, so underlying floor joists cannot be inspected for damage.

Staircase
Its construction and state of repair.

Damp-Proof Course
Whether one is present – some pre-1880 properties were not built with a damp-proof course (*see below*). If there is one, does it appear to be working

correctly, ascertained by visible signs of damp and/or moisture-meter test results? However, moisture meters do have limitations, and in certain circumstances can sometimes give false readings (*see* Chapter 6).

Air Vents/Air-bricks
For underfloor ventilation of timber floors; where these are situated and if they are adequate and not blocked or covered.

Large, steel air-brick, with tile DPC beneath and tiling above to seal outside air from the cavity above and direct it to underfloor cavity.

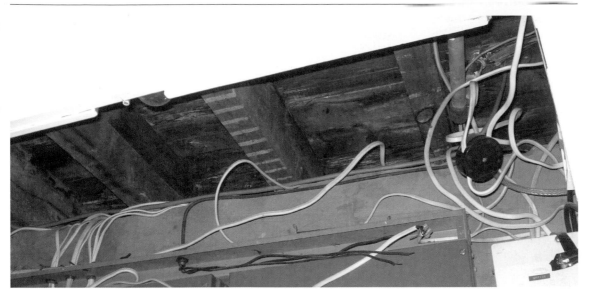

Dangerous electrical wiring in a ceiling cavity – other electrical problems are very likely.
Roy Ilott & Associates Ltd

Woodworm/Fungal Attack, Wood Rot
Any evidence of the above and, if so, if it appears to be active or merely evidence of a past attack.

Internal Decoration
General comments; presence of any cracks in wall or ceiling plaster.

Fittings and Finishes
Serviceability of WC, sinks, baths and so on.

Services

Central Heating
Stating the kind of system, type of boiler, whether it is adequate and functioning correctly.

Cold-Water Supply, Hot-Water System
Assessment of storage tanks (usually in the roof space), supply pipes and domestic hot-water cylinder.

Electrical Installation
This can only be a superficial inspection, since wiring is mostly beneath floors or hidden within ceilings and walls. A surveyor will normally look at the consumer unit and main supply meter, and make a comment on whether the visible wiring looks adequate. If he or she sees any old, fabric-and-rubber covered cables, or ceramic fuse boxes, this indicates that wiring is definitely dangerous and pre-1950, requiring urgent overall replacement. If there are any visible suspicions that the wiring contravenes regulations or looks dangerous, the surveyor will recommend a complete survey by a suitably qualified electrician. (*See Chapter 10*)

These cables in a kitchen wall recess may not be live. On the other hand they could be carrying current and potentially deadly – get them checked by a qualified electrician before going near them.

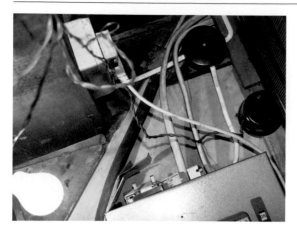

A hotch-potch of dangerous looking electrical wiring in an understairs cupboard.

Gas Supply
As above, the surveyor is not qualified to make the necessary tests. So if he suspects gas piping or that appliances need attention, he'll recommend an inspection by an engineer who is on the Gas Safe Register (*see* Chapter 10).

Rainwater Drainage
Visual, ground-level inspection of the state of the gutters, downpipes and drainage gulleys. And if it can be ascertained, whether rainwater discharges to a soakaway or the main drainage system.

Soil Drainage and Fittings
These are checked to see that water from sinks and baths and WCs runs away adequately. Again, if a drainage fault is suspected, a qualified plumber's inspection is recommended.

Other Areas

Outside
Whether there are outbuildings, e.g. greenhouses, sheds, garages, etc. What these are made of, their general condition. The condition and construction of boundary walls, fences and gates.

This plastic gutter has lost its support and is bowing dangerously.

Having a Building Survey

Tips and Checkpoints

- It is important to find a surveyor who has experience of your type and age of property. The Royal Institution of Chartered Surveyors can give recommendations.
- Do not feel obliged to use the surveyor recommended by your building society – he may not be acquainted with your particular type of property.
- Consider choosing a small surveyors' practice, rather than a large, impersonal organization. You are likely to get a more personal, efficient service and you will be able to talk to the person who actually did your survey.
- If your lender insists on an HSV survey, pay for this separately; then, if you think it necessary, commission your own Building Survey: this is because, if your building society is made aware of faults, they may withhold funds in the light of these – it's therefore up to them to make their own checks.
- Bear in mind the limitations of a Building Survey. If you want carpets to be lifted or for drains to be professionally tested, these examinations will have to be agreed with the vendor, and will cost you more.
- Read the report carefully, not simply the summary. Do not hesitate to contact the surveyor afterwards to discuss anything you do not understand.
- Prior to exchanging contracts, obtain quotations from several reputable builders for the required works.

Warnings

- If you plan to buy a house that has been professionally treated for wood rot or woodworm, the company's guarantee passes to you as the new owner, for however long the period of guarantee runs. However, this guarantee only applies to the actual timbers that the company has treated, nothing else. So, if any timber in the same room develops rot or decay, it is not covered by the guarantee. And check that the company is still trading: if it has ceased to operate, the guarantee is invalid.
- Accept that for a pre-1700 building, you may have to put up with a degree of rising damp, and will need to regularly open windows to encourage ventilation.
- If there's an extension, conservatory or loft-conversion, make absolutely certain that the local authority has granted permission for this, and that there is something in writing from them to state that the addition has been built in accordance with building regulations. If not, you can apply for retrospective permission and may get it, but it's a gamble; or extra building works may be needed in order to get retrospective permission. If you buy somewhere that hasn't got the local authority's approval for such changes, any future sale may be blighted. Remember, even if your local authority grants retrospective planning permission, the building will still need to comply with current building regulations, possibly requiring more work.
- Beware of obvious botched jobs and obviously new paintwork, which may conceal problems (*see* Chapter 7).
- Flooding is not confined to riverbank areas, and nowadays increasing numbers of homes are being designated as being within a flood plain (*see* Chapter 6. Ground water can ooze from chalk valleys, lapping around foundations, and will not dry out for months if the water table is very high.
- If a flat roof has been patch-repaired, check on the ceiling beneath. If this has not been replaced, there's the possibility that damaging water may still be trapped inside.
- Remember that an old building, even in good condition, is likely to need perpetual maintenance, so budget for this.

Expert Quote

An experienced surveyor advises:

If you see things that are bodged, one loses confidence because you wonder what has been bodged that's invisible, say under the floorboards. If I see bad detailing I think, 'Well if they can't do something right that's visible, what messes are there out of sight?' If you see obviously botched jobs, such as dangerous-looking electrical wiring in the understairs cupboard, it's a sure bet that what you can't see – under floorboards or in the loft – is going to be an absolute disaster. Steer clear of such houses.

What you're really bringing into play is the experience of, and knowledge of, a surveyor, which is why it's important to make sure you're getting somebody who is experienced. Problem areas in old houses are the parts that are getting worn out, and this may not necessarily be apparent. Electric wiring is a classic case, as are roof tiles and rendering. Also, with an old property there may be some bungled previous repairs that appear satisfactory but that can actually cause a problem later – for instance, when people bridge the DPC (damp-proof course) when building a nice patio. Our problem in doing a survey is that you are conscious that you're intruding on someone else's house, and if the purchaser decides not to buy it for whatever reason, they could say that the survey wasn't satisfactory. But if you've done some damage to the house in the course of inspection, who is going to pay to put things right?

Roof Space

State of the timbers, the apparent condition of underside of slates or tiles. Is there evidence of sag or overloading, or of removal of necessary structural roof support timbers?

Summary

Outlining what the surveyor was unable to test. The surveyor's opinion of the condition of the property as a whole. Possibly recommendations or otherwise as to whether the property is worth the agreed price. Judgements as to future likely repairs that may be needed. Any additional considerations, e.g. if the property is a flat, the extent of liability for the common parts, such as stairways, halls and roofs. The presence of asbestos (*see* Chapter 7), in whatever form, is always commented on, with recommendations as to whether it should be professionally removed, left alone or painted to seal its surface.

Finally, it may include a list of jobs to be done immediately and work recommended to be done in the foreseeable future, in order of importance, as well as information on any likely restriction to the envisaged work from the local authority's point of view.

Kit for Doing Surveys

- Bradawl, pocket knife, cold chisel, hammer, pliers.
- Electrical moisture meter – can be hired; this is a probe that measures moisture content in walls and timbers, and works by measuring electrical conductivity.
- Builder's spirit-level, 1m long, for checking that walls are upright or not.
- Magnifying glass for examining fungi on timber.
- Flexible steel tape-measure.
- Ladder, if you plan to go on a roof – but be aware that there are safety issues here.
- Safety helmet for dangerous sites.
- Camera and flash unit.
- Field glasses, so you can look at roofs from ground level.
- Powerful electric torch.
- Notepad or portable voice recorder or laptop, for making notes.

CAN YOU DO YOUR OWN SURVEY?

In theory you can, and, as stated above, it makes sense to take a good look at a building yourself before going to the expense of paying for a professional Building Survey.

POTENTIALLY SERIOUS PROBLEMS OF OLDER HOUSES

Cavity Wall-Tie Failure

Where the metal bridging ties used in cavity walls corrode, resulting in movement of the walls (see Chapter 5).

Look for: horizontal cracks in brickwork every six to eight courses, caused by the metal corroding within the wall, and consequently expanding and cracking the surrounding material. Also look for walls that are bulging or leaning outwards.

Subsidence

Where the building is cracking up due to ground movement (see Chapter 5).

Look for: diagonal or tapering cracks, with the widest edge at the top, often at the corner of the house at the top or end of a wall, or around doorways or windows, a dip on horizontal coursing of stone or brick, or sloping lintels.

Broken or Bridged Damp-Proof Course (DPC)

When the building's defence against damp rising up the walls breaks down (see Chapter 6).

Look for: a line of black (slate or bitumen material) or differently coloured brick along a horizontal brick course, around 15cm (6in) above ground level. Make sure that debris, soil or similar is not concealing parts of this, as this means water is likely to penetrate the walls, where it can cause damage. For a rendered wall, there should be a break in the render at DPC level, or a special angled bead to facilitate this break; however, since a break in rendering can be concealed with paint, this may be hard to spot. Very often patios or paths are built, which raise the ground level so that the DPC is bridged, and you'll have to budget for dismantling these and lowering the ground level. 1930s houses

in particular often had a skirt of rendering at the base, and it's important that, if this is damaged, it is repaired or removed, as water can enter through the cracks and bridge the DPC.

Window- and Door-Frame Woodwork/Metalwork Decay or Rot

Look for: obvious rot and decay; old metal windows are likely to be rusty, especially if their paintwork is compromised.

Expert Quote

Architect Julian Owen, of Julian Owen Associates, advises:

> Be systematic. Have a mental checklist in your mind when you look at the basic structure, any obvious tiles missing, or if the roof's ridge line is starting to slump. Walk around the whole property rather than just looking at the rooms. The most obvious signal of trouble is the smell – a damp problem or rots leave a particular smell in the air. Look at the roof and walls, then inside look at ceilings, each wall and each floor, going through each room systematically. By doing this you are more likely to spot the things that don't leap out obviously, because people normally will try to conceal bits, so that they look better than they are. The roof's ridge line is important: the main timbers, and ceiling and roof joists start to rot at their feet, so they drop, giving you a wobbly line instead of a straight one. When timber contained within a wall rots you get the wall starting to bow outwards, or can sometimes tell by the line of the wall, or see evidence of remedial work that's been done. Unfortunately on a first visit you can't start lifting carpets or floorboards. Go through things systematically, making sure you've looked at everything.

In addition to running a busy architectural practice, Julian is also an author of a number of books. The following excellent titles of his are available from Crowood: *Conservatories* (2005), *The Complete Loft-conversion Book* (2010), *Kit and Modern Timber-framed Houses* (2007) and *Managing Home Alterations and Extension Projects* (2012).

Rotten timber windowsill.

These cracks in outside rendering are drawing in moisture by capillary action, though they don't suggest major problems such as subsidence.

Look for: bulges under paintwork, indicating expansion caused by rust.

Ground Surface in Front of Walls at the Wrong Level

This can encourage dampness to rise up the walls.

Look for: Is the ground sloping away from the house as it should be, or does it slope towards the building? The presence of pools of un-dispersed rainwater could mean the drainage is insufficient, and requires further investigation.

Exterior Rendering Cracks and Damage

Look for: cracking and splits, particularly if it's in one part only, which could mean that non-matching mortar, or mortar with a high cement-to-sand ratio has been used. However, splits in rendering are quite common and usually do not indicate a major fault, but if left unattended for a long period can allow water to enter the fabric of the wall and do damage.

Decay of Internal Timber Lintels Above Door and Window Openings

Supportive lintels hold up the brickwork above these openings, and internal timber, used in the past before concrete/metal lintels became the norm, frequently rots within the wall.

Look for: any sagging of brickwork or stonework above windows or doors.

Stonework Problems

Look for: splintering or spalling (swelling).

Brickwork Decay

Look for: any obvious erosion or different type of surface, to indicate that the bricks' outer skin has been compromised ('blown') allowing water into the wall.

Differential Settlement

This can occur when an extension has been added to a building, because the new part's

Large crack in a stone step.

movement drags the remainder with it. It is structural movement that can occur when a modern extension with conventional (deep) foundations is added to buildings with shallow foundations.

Look for: splits or cracks along the joint line between old and new structures.

Nail Sickness

Where the nails holding roof tiles or slates have corroded, allowing these items to slide down the roof.

Look for: any rows of roof coverings that appear to be out of true or sliding downwards.

Overloading/Sagging

When concrete or clay tiles are used to replace light slates, the timber supports beneath in the roof space, which were not designed to support this extra weight, can bend or break down as a consequence. Similar problems occur when supportive roof timbers are removed, for instance when an illegal loft-conversion is done.

Look for: collapse or curving of the ridge line, or any sign of irregular external roof appearance.

Dry Rot, Wet Rot

Fungal attacks that destroy timber (*see* Chapter 8).

Woodworm, or Other Timber Infestation Attack

Apparent as holes in the timber's surface, especially underneath stairs, or in other unvarnished/unpainted areas (*see* Chapter 8).

Interstitial Condensation

When timber is subjected to dampness that cannot evaporate, and consequently rots (*see* Chapter 6).

WHAT TO LOOK FOR

Roof

Most roofs can be viewed from ground level, using binoculars or field glasses, as necessary.

- Dips and depressions (sagging) along the tile surface. Sagging can often be unimportant, but could indicate joist decay or even overloading.
- Roof spread, due to inadequate supportive timbers, either because of timber's decay or overloading.

Several slates in this roof have slipped out of line, which could indicate nail sickness.

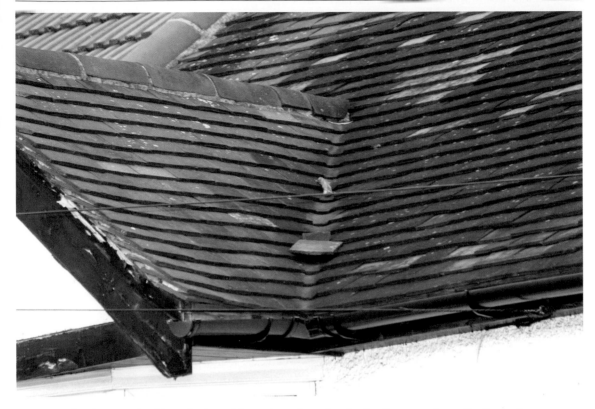

A reasonably healthy looking tiled roof, but where has the single tile come from that's resting along the valley?

- Abutments between slates/tiles and chimneys — is there lead flashing, and does it look undamaged? These areas may be filled with mortar, which is unlikely to be successful in the long term, as the material is prone to cracking when bridging two surfaces.
- Missing, broken or slipping tiles or slates.
- Vegetation growth in roof valleys.
- Blocked gutters, which can cause water overflow onto the wall: excessive soaking can go right through the wall, apparent as a damp patch.
- Chimneys: do they lean as if they are unsafe? Check whether the flaunching into which pots are bedded is cracked.
- Eaves line: look for broken gutters, blocked downpipe hopper heads, rotten fascia boards, rafter ends and wall plates. Ensure there's a double thickness of tiles or slates (soakers underneath) at the eaves.

- Ridge tiles: check for broken or slipping tiles and assess the condition of the pointing.
- Parapet walls on Georgian buildings: assess their integrity and also make sure that the gutters they conceal are functioning properly.
- Barge boards and purlin ends: check for decay.
- Dormer windows: make sure that where they join the main roof appears undamaged.
- Flat roofs: search for puddles of standing water on flat roofs, as this can indicate a potential area of weakness, and prolonged lakes can find entry into the roof's structure.
- Patched repairs: tiles or slates that look different to the rest.

In the Roof Space

- *Look for:* roof timbers that are unexpectedly foreshortened, which suggests that they have been recently cut, particularly where there's a loft-conversion.

- Examine the structural integrity of roof timbers, particularly underneath water tanks and water pipes.
- Note: old timbers can often have a whitish tinge on the outside, which is similar to the appearance of dry rot, but is often simply plaster it has been in contact with, usually above a lath-and-plaster ceiling.
- Any loft-conversion should conform to building regulations and have the requisite planning permission. The roof can collapse if insufficient support is provided, walls can also be forced to lean outwards, and there are special fire regulations to be met.
- Assess the condition of gable walls and chimney stacks.
- *Look for:* any entry of water during rainfall, indicating missing or damaged tiles.
- Examine the underside of tiles, if they are visible (there may be timber boarding and/or felt blocking your view). Tiles can deteriorate from the underside while appearing in good condition from above.

External Walls

- Diagonal or tapering cracks, with widest edge at the top, particularly at the corner of house, or top or end of wall, or around doorways and windows, or a noticeable dip in horizontal coursing of stone of brick, either of which could indicate subsidence. However, if the latter occurs over doors or windows it could mean decaying timber lintels within the wall.
- Horizontal cracks in brickwork, every six to eight courses, which could indicate cavity wall-tie failure.
- Walls bulging or leaning, which could indicate subsidence or cavity wall-tie failure.
- Visible lintels – check to see if these are sloping.
- Damp-proof course – look for strips of black slate, black tiles or differently coloured brick about 3 to 6in above ground level. Make sure that debris or brick is not covering any part of this. For rendered properties the edge of the DPC should not be covered by render, but is likely to be painted, and therefore impossible to see.
- Window and doorframe joinery and/or metalwork. Is there rot or rust? Old metal Critall windows (1930s to 1950s) are especially prone to rust at their hinges.
- Area of ground in front of walls: Is it flat, does it slope away from the house? Or does the ground slope towards the walls, thereby encouraging ground water.
- Exterior rendering – cracks and crevices are usual and, unless specially noticeable, are usually of no significance; however, they do need attention.
- Doors and windows: is stonework or brickwork sagging visibly above them? If so it could mean that an internal timber lintel is rotted.
- Timber-framed buildings: examine carefully where infilling areas join timbers, as decay often occurs at this point.
- Stone buildings – look carefully for splintering or spalling, particularly around windows, as often iron is embedded in stone around these.
- Air-bricks/air-vents – are these blocked, or partly covered by soil or debris?
- Tiled or tile-clad walls – check for the same problems as occur in roofs.
- New extensions – make sure there is no cracking where these join the original house.
- Messy repointing or differently coloured bricks, indicating a repair.
- Old cast-iron pipes and guttering tends to rust at the back, where they sometimes lack protective paint, so check these areas carefully.

Internal Walls

- Horizontal cracking, coupled with lifting floors and ceilings, which could indicate subsidence.
- Cracked, flaking areas of plasterwork, which could be indicative of dampness.
- Bulging areas, which could indicate movement or plaster that's lost adherence to the wall.
- Damp, decay or mould.
- Cracks between walls, floors or ceilings.
- Areas over doorways or windows – are there appreciable cracks or splits, which could indicate failure of an internal lintel? Alternatively, a sloping lintel could indicate subsidence.
- Powdery crystalline salt-line tidemark band up to 1m (3ft) from the floor, below which there's flaking plaster – a classic sign of rising damp.
- Dampness, with mould apparent, most notable behind items of furniture, often in a ceil-

ing corner, or beads of moisture on hard shiny surfaces. All these are symptoms of condensation.

- Damp areas apparent only during wet weather – indicating penetrating damp, that comes straight through the wall.

Timber Floors

- Fungus and fruiting bodies, on or underneath floor cavities, meaning wet or dry rots (*see* Chapter 5).
- Presence of tiny (or larger) holes on the timber's surface, often more prevalent on the undersides of timber items, which are unpainted or unvarnished. This indicates wood-boring insects (*see* Chapter 5).
- Is the floor slanting? Check with a spirit-level, as this can suggest subsidence.
- As you walk, do you feel the floor 'bounce'? This can mean decay of the joists beneath.
- Gaps between skirtings and floorboards, possibly indicating subsidence.
- Obviously recently renewed timber, which may indicate a past attack of timber decay, so check other areas carefully.
- Bathroom and WC room floors should be checked carefully for dampness or rot, as plumbing leaks can engender rot over a long period and are often not noticed.

- Skirting boards should be checked, especially for woodworm holes.

Other Areas

- Concrete floors – lift any covering lino, as, if the surface is damp, it means there's no damp-proof membrane in or below the screed, so the water from the soil is rising straight up from the earth.
- Woodworm should be searched for in the understairs cupboard, where there are plenty of unpainted undersides of timbers, as well as under the shelving in old larders.
- Blocked drains – if you have any doubts, commission a CCTV survey.
- Cracked paving or drives, which could indicate subsidence.

Services/Heating Systems

- Poor ventilation of boilers, fires and stoves.
- Obviously untidy electrical services or wiring that's clearly been done in an amateur way.
- Bear in mind that many of the old gas mains leading from the meter into the house are undersized for modern-day gas usage and may need to be replaced.
- Old central heating systems were often badly designed and may need completely updating.

CHAPTER 2

Different Kinds of Building and Living Beyond the Mains

The key features of buildings of different historical eras are listed here.

TUDOR/STUART 1400s TO 1714

Many are timber-framed and some may have an overhang of the upper storey over the lower, called a jetty; thicker timbers denote greater age, as does the closeness together of the timbers. After 1590, houses were more likely to be built from brick or stone.

Roofs. Plain, with a steep pitch, two planes supported by gable walls; later roofs were hipped (see Chapter 4).

Chimneys. Either central or a third of the way along the elevation.

Staircases. On the chimney-breast, against a side wall or, in early houses, could be external.

Windows. The earliest windows were called leaded lights (see Chapter 4), the area subdivided by strips of lead, to join the small 'quarries' of glass, because this was the maximum area of glass that could be produced. Later on, window

Tudor houses in Strand Street, Sandwich – the timber structure has moved dramatically, yet the buildiing is perfectly habitable.

Another view of Strand Street, Sandwich, showing the 'Sandwich Weavers' historic sign on one building, dated 1500.

glass was divided by wood or stone verticals. Sash windows were first used around 1685.

Doorways. Sometimes these had a hood with a decorated canopy over it.

GEORGIAN 1714–1811

Most Georgian architecture is symmetrical, almost mathematically precise. Stone was used to frame windows and doorways, and as decorative cornerstones (quoins). Stucco covered inferior brickwork, or was used to mimic stone, as in false ashlaring. Coade stone was used after 1769 (*see* Chapter 9). After 1750 bow-fronted houses were common.

Roofs. Pitch was less steep than previously, and symmetrical chimney-stacks were usual. Mansard roofs were popular.

Windows. Usually sash, with decorative lintels above. Wooden frames became more slender throughout the century.

Doorways. These were frequently approached by steps with wrought-iron banisters. Doors were of pine and divided into six panels with carved mouldings and fanlights.

Interiors. The entire first floor was sometimes called the 'piano nobile', and used for entertaining. This era had interiors with a lot of decorative plasterwork, which was particularly flamboyant prior to 1760.

REGENCY/LATE GEORGIAN 1811–37

Jacobean and Elizabethan styles were in vogue. Plain brickwork or stucco was used to contrast with elaborate doorcases, eaves and windows. Porches

Georgian houses in Brighton.

Terrace of Georgian houses in Brighton.

ABOVE: **Beautiful wrought-iron balcony on a Georgian house.**

RIGHT: **Lovely steps up to a front door, laid with encaustic tiles.**

had ironwork frames and cast-iron balconies, and window boxes were popular.

Roofs. These were shallow pitched, with eaves projecting out from the wall.

Windows. Wider with slim glazing bars.

VICTORIAN/EDWARDIAN 1837–1910

Typical Victorian style can be a mixture of revivals of previous styles: Gothic, Greek Revival, Tudor Rococo and Italianate. There were many terraces in towns and spacious 'villas' in suburban or country areas. Pugin was one of this era's greatest exponents, and he spearheaded the Gothic revival style, and the new concept of designing a house from 'the inside out', planning rooms and their shapes rather than deciding on the exterior shape and working inwards, as was done previously. Brick of differing colours was used a lot, as well as blue slate for roofs. Doorways were frequently recessed to form integral porches.

'Villa' style of Victorian house.

Good, solidly built Victorian or Edwardian house.

Roofs. Gables were emblazed with mock-timber framing and decorated with overhanging eaves supported by brackets. These often had carved bargeboards, and areas of different coloured and shaped tiles to form a pattern (fish scaled, diamonds etc) and elaborate ridge tiles. Neo-gothic roofs had turrets, towers and spires.

Windows. After 1845 large sheets of glass could be made, therefore no glazing bars were required. Sash or mullion windows were ubiquitous, with bays topped by a castellated parapet or balustrade. This was the heyday of stained and painted glass.

Interiors. High ceilings, with chair-height dado rails above lincrusta wallpaper or wooden panelling. Impressive staircases and ornamental plasterwork was usual.

Magnificent portico to Victorian or Edwardian house.

Architectural Styles

Gothic revival, 1750–1885
Leading designers: Batty Langley, Horace Walpole and Pugin.
The last thirty years defined as 'High Victorian Gothic'. This is a basic gothic style that incorporates features such as stained glass, battened doors and elegantly pillared windows.

Art Nouveau, 1880s to 1914
Leading designers: John Ruskin and Rennie Mackintosh.
This style originated in France (translated as 'New Art'). This is a decorative, rather than an architectural, style, described as an attempt to break away from the eclectic revivalist tastes of the Victorian era. The emphasis is on craftsmanship and associated industries, the principle philosophy being modernism, using new, fresh, non-derivative idea. It features sinuous lines, curves, luxuriant foliage and women with long flowing hair, and designs were consciously asymmetrical.

Arts and Crafts, 1885 to 1930s
Leading designers: William Morris and Edward Barnsley.
This approach to design was intended as a 'rural' look, even when used in towns. Cottages would usually have a combined kitchen and dining area plus sitting room, and three upstairs bedrooms. Pebbledash, plain roof tiles and casement windows typify Arts and Crafts buildings.

Art Deco, 1925 to 1930s
Taking its name from the *'Exposition Internationale des Arts Decoratifs et Industriels Modernes'* in Paris in 1925, Art Deco features bold geometric shapes and stylised natural forms and also encompassed furniture. Art Deco buildings tend to be simple, clean and full of light. There are touches of intense colour, ornamental glass and tiles or paint used to accentuate larger white or pale textured surfaces to contrast with plain materials. Walls are often curving or even rounded.

Building Innovations

1590s onwards: chimneys were in general use.
16th century: glazed windows first used and bricks were becoming more popular.
1580s: roof tiles were used generally.
1630: dormer windows were invented.
1650: doors with two panels became popular. It was realized that timber building joists had more tensile strength when laid on edge, rather than flat, as they had been used previously.
1685: the sash window was invented.
1700: panelled doors had six, eight or ten panels and fanlights arrived.
17th century: wallpaper was used in affluent homes.
1750: bow-fronted houses were growing in numbers.
1769: Coade stone became generally available.
18th century: there were wider front doors with windows either side and porches.
1800s onwards: the arrival of the semi-detached house and vertical sash windows.
1820s: corridors were introduced.
1830s: central heating utilizing hot water was invented.
1840s: roof eaves were shortened.
1845: removal of the tax on glass, meaning more windows were used.
1850s: glass could be made in large sheets, meaning window bars were no longer necessary.
1875: basements were not always incorporated into homes as a standard feature.
1890s: electric light was invented.

Terrace houses, c.1880.

DIFFERENT TYPES OF HOUSES

Terrace Houses

These developed in Georgian times and evolved during the Victorian period, when building regulations became more stringent. Terraces are continuous rows of houses with open spaces at front and back, ranging from the wonderful Georgian terraces of Bath or Brighton to the crowded 'back-to-back' terraces in industrial towns. Double-fronted houses have an entrance in the centre of the façade with a room either side; alternatively, there could be 'front doors adjoining' or 'front doors alternating with ground-floor room windows'. Early terrace houses had basements and semi-basements; later on there were often back extensions of one or two storeys. During the late-nineteenth century, a typical layout would be a ground floor with two rooms and a scullery, and two or three bedrooms upstairs. Construction was usually of load-bearing external walls and internal load-bearing cross walls, with two rooms per floor, divided by partitions. Sometimes there were bay windows on the ground floor, occasionally also on the first floor. Dividing walls were commonly only a single-brick thick (100mm/4in). Properties on the ends of terraces can suffer from the 'Bookend Effect', whereby they lean sideways as a result of lateral forces within the terrace as a whole: one cause can be if everyone in the terrace removes their central room dividing wall to create an open-plan downstairs, then the loss of this central support can leave the entire structure subject to such movement: a 'pushing outwards' towards the

---

Expert Quote

An experienced solicitor advises:

Sometimes in a terrace, one property can have an upper storey arched section extending across an alley owned by someone else. This is called a 'flying freehold' and some mortgage lenders can be wary of these. Legally you always should have an 'easement', meaning that the overhanging part of your house has a right to be there and the right to have the necessary structural support.

ends. Symptoms of the bookend effect can be vertical cracks between each property. Foundations of early terraced houses are often extremely shallow, leading to a possibility of subsidence.

Semi-Detached

This is the most common property type, accounting for 32 per cent of UK housing transactions in 2008. These are pairs of houses built side-by-side with a party wall in between, normally so that each is a mirror image of the other. They were developed during the 1800s when father and son architects, John Shaw Senior and Junior, designed the first semi-detached houses in Chalk Farm, North London. Semis were typical of the middle-class driven suburban building boom of the 1920s and 1930s. Influences include Art Deco, with 'mock-Tudor' and 'Chalet' styles. After 1945, many council houses were also semis. They are likely to have a driveway or garage for parking, bay windows at the front and French windows leading onto the rear garden. Semis were the first type of houses to have indoor toilets and tiled bathrooms as standard.

Detached

This does not share an inside wall with any other house, and its outside walls don't touch anyone else. Types can range from a small cottage up to a large mansion, and include bungalows and villas: in the late 1800s and early 1900s the term villa developed to describe a freestanding, comfortable house, usually in the suburbs.

Typical semi-detached suburban house in south London, c.1930s.

Lovely stained-glass windows like this were sometimes a feature of 1930s houses.

Cottage

The definition of a cottage is a 'small house or habitation without land'. While a cottage is often considered to be a small, detached dwelling in a rural location, and typically of traditional build, it can also mean a modern construction, built to resemble a traditional building. The term originated from homes for agricultural workers, meaning 'dwelling of a cotter'. Traditionally, the term tends to refer to older dwellings, and cottages can also be semi-detached or terraced, and a cottage can actually be a substantial house. Typically, they are vernacular buildings displaying the local colours of stone, brick or tile.

THE AMENITY SOCIETIES

These organizations are charities, which also perform a statutory function for English Heritage and CADW, who manage the listed buildings throughout England and Wales, respectively. Termed 'statutory consultees', they also work with local authorities (LAs) – when LAs or individuals apply to alter, demolish or extend listed buildings, the relevant organization must legally be consulted for their advice.

Their main function is to protect buildings from damage and destruction, and to encourage their care. All welcome new members, no expertise is needed to join and charges are nominal. If you have an old house, it's a way of accessing detailed information, getting expert advice and taking part in courses and social events. Amenity societies exist to help their members look after their homes. Many of them produce useful technical information and leaflets, and offer courses in practical and historical aspects pertaining to their period of architecture.

THE SOCIETY FOR THE PROTECTION OF ANCIENT BUILDINGS (SPAB)

(www.spab.co.uk; 020 7377 1644)

Period of Buildings Covered: Prior to 1720
SPAB was founded in 1877 by William Morris and others as part of their crusade to defend old buildings against destruction and damaging restoration, brought about by the Industrial Revolution and expansion of building programmes, and the 'new' and much faster and partially mechanized building techniques and materials. Morris and SPAB established the system of 'listing' buildings so as to give them legal protection from damage by their owners. SPAB's guiding philosophy is to follow Morris's original manifesto, including the belief that old buildings should be skilfully repaired, rather than restored. Nowadays this translates into finding practical and positive ways to care for old buildings. There are eighteen regional groups throughout the country.

What They Offer
Huge source for technical information, including a Technical Advice line (Monday to Thursday mornings: 020 7456 0916). Courses on a variety of subjects for professionals and homeowners. Bookshop, excellent and detailed technical leaflets. Lectures, guided visits to private houses, social and educational events, plus a list of properties for sale in need of repair. Also a very active Mills section, for owners and enthusiasts of these structures. Genuinely friendly, likeable and helpful staff.

Douglas Kent, Technical Director of SPAB says:

We're a bit different to the other amenity societies, in that we're able to tackle technical matters,
and offer an advice telephone line, plus specialist
courses for contractors and homeowners. A basic
tenet of our work is to repair rather than restore
whenever practical. When a homeowner tells me
how our advice has solved their problem, that
absolutely makes my day – I feel as if all my efforts
are worthwhile.

Georgian Group

(www.georgiangroup.org.uk; 087 1750 2936 or 020
7529 8924)

Period of Buildings Covered: 1700–1840
This national society campaigns against the neglect,
maltreatment and destruction of Georgian architecture, parks and gardens, and promotes the
appreciation and enjoyment of them, using an
active programme of education and publications.
Founded in 1937 with the aim to battle the demolition, disfigurement and neglect of Georgian
buildings. Over 40 per cent of all listed houses in
the country date from this era. Described as 'a
vibrant and growing community with more than
3,300 members'.

What They Offer
An annual newsletter and journal, colour magazine, huge collection of publications, very good
technical leaflets and books (discounted for
members), lectures, study days, visits to private
buildings, foreign study tours, an annual sympo-
sium and technical query service. There is a
members' library with adjoining club room in
central London.
Robert Bargery, of the Georgian Group, says:

All projects, whether major or minor, are fascinating to me. While the major country houses
such as Chatsworth House and Blenheim Palace
are wonderful to be associated with, I am especially keen to expand our work to include the un-
celebrated Georgian terraces, for instance in
run-down areas like Dalston and Hackney, in
London.

The Victorian Society

(www.victoriansociety.org.uk; 020 7529 8924)

Period of Buildings Covered: 1837–1914
Colloquially referred to as VICSOC, it began in
1957 in London, with the aim to study and protect
Victorian and Edwardian architecture and other
arts. The head office is in London and there are eight
regional groups throughout the country. Founder
members included Sir John Betjeman and Niklaus
Pevsner. A fairly political organization, VICSOC
campaigns to conserve buildings from destruction,
and aims to awaken public interest in, the appreciation and study of, arts, architecture, crafts, design
and social history of that era. Described as 'The
Champion for Victorian and Edwardian architecture in England and Wales'.

What They Offer
Summer school, courses, lectures, tri-annual magazine *The Victorian*, books, booklets, visits, confer-
ences and day schools.
Ian Dungavell, director of the Victorian Society,
says:

I was stunned to discover that in the sixties
people wanted to demolish St Pancras Station, and
I thought what a horrendous loss it would have
been if an organization such as ours had not been
fighting for it. When you're saving a building you
feel like a doctor wrenching a dying patient back
from the brink. It's very often the Victorian buildings that supply the character and feel of different
places, and people regard such constructions as
background to their daily lives, and feel devastated
when they disappear. A huge part of our work is
constructive, giving sensible practical advice and
help on adapting old buildings for new uses.

The Twentieth Century Society

(www.c20society.org.uk; 020 7250 3857)

*Period of Buildings Covered: 1914 to Present
Day (Including the Twenty-First Century!)*
This evolved from the Thirties Society, established
in 1979 as a result of a meeting of architects and
conservationists at the Park Lane Hotel Piccadilly
in London. Renamed in 1995, in accordance with
the later periods of buildings being looked after. Its

principle aims are to safeguard the period's heritage of architecture and design, through education and conservation. Many activities are handled by volunteers, and new recruits are always welcome.

What They Offer
Varied and lively events, including hosted visits to private homes. Guided visits to foreign cities. Lectures, tri-annual magazine *Journal of Twentieth Century Architecture*, also leaflets, publications and books.

LIVING BEYOND MAINS' SERVICES

If you decide to buy a house way out in the wilds, which is not connected to mains' services, you first of all need to know the practicalities regarding the basic necessities: water supply, drainage, electricity, gas (not vital) and vehicle access. Costs of connection of services relate directly to the proximity of the supplier's closest connection, usually the nearest village. Service providers always want new customers, so will be happy to assess connection costs for you. Electricity is supplied to practically all of the UK, apart from outlying areas of Wales and Scotland. Gas is not so widely available, but there are good alternatives for running heating: electricity, liquid petroleum gas (LPG), oil and solid fuel. There are also alternative sources for waste-water disposal and water supplies, if connection is very costly or impractical. It's worth bearing in mind that conventional suppliers' services are always the easiest and cheapest option as regards running costs, meaning that initial outlay for connection to these could be recouped in years to come, rather than using less conventional alternatives.

If your building is listed (*see* Chapter 3), your local Conservation Officer is likely to be flexible regarding Listed Building Consent, since local authorities would rather have listed buildings occupied and cared for, and recognize the practicalities of needing basic services. Remember also that good security measures are absolutely vital, since an isolated house is a prime target for thieves.

Road Access
First, find out if the house is approached across someone else's land. Rights of way over someone

---

Mains' Services

Electricity
Supply cables run underground or overhead on pylons (more usual in outlying locations). Approach your chosen supplier, who can arrange with a distributor to make a connection, or you can go direct to a distributor.

Gas
You can go direct to a gas supplier, details of all of them on the ofgem website (www. ofgem.gov.uk; 020 77901 7295). In this case, the chosen gas supplier will manage he entire process. Alternatively, you can contact the National Grid directly (www.nationalgrid. com/uk; 0870 903 9999). National Grid manages the process of installing or altering the gas pipe to your home, from initial enquiry to completion of the works.

Water
Contact the water-supply company for your area, who will quote you a price based on the building's location, size and number of storeys.

Drainage
Again, contact the water-supply company. Their connection cost depends on the nearness of the public sewer.

---

else's land should be stated in the deeds of both houses, and if they are not, clarification is essential. Remember that the neighbour(s) may have rights of way over your land as well. Should trees obstruct your proposed route to the house on your own land, check with the local authority that none are covered by Tree Preservation Orders, as, if so, it will be illegal to remove them.

Motorways and major trunk roads are the responsibility of the Highways Agency, while smaller public roads are under the jurisdiction of the local authority Highways Department. Private access roads are described by local authorities as 'not adopted', and are not controlled by the local authority and a small contractor can construct this kind of approach route for a single house, provided that certain criteria are met – for instance, the earth has to have a minimum bearing capacity. However, a private road has to be linked to the public highway, and only a larger contractor, who has adequate insurance cover (to cover the possibility of a road accident, cutting through utility cables, etc.), will be allowed to do this part of the work. If your proposed access road is larger and/or has to be shared with other people, it will ultimately be deemed a 'public' road, and the local authority needs to be involved at the outset; they will do soil-bearing tests and stipulate the depth of stone and thickness of tarmac, and ultimately they will have to 'adopt' it.

Practically, the builder or structural engineer needs to have knowledge of local soil conditions to calculate the depth of foundations for the road; this is based on the weight of vehicles your road needs to cater for: remember, if you're having major building work done on the house, heavy lorries are going to visit. A typical construction might involve an excavation of 30–60cm (1–2ft), lined with heavy geotextile membrane, a material made to stop the insurgence of mud and to keep the structure in place. The first layer of road is called 'formation' 100mm (4in) diameter pieces of clean stone, followed by finer grade stone. Finally, there is a layer of 'type one': stone particles from 40mm (1½in) down to dust. An alternative might be a base of reclaimed brick hardcore from a demolition site, blinded off with 'type one'. The top surface can be gravel, block paving, tarmac or asphalt. The road needs to be slightly cambered for drainage, and the drained water has to be directed to soakaways around the site – this water cannot enter the main drains. It's also necessary to consider how to preserve the edges – block paving kerbs might be a suitable edging.

Private Water Supply

Water can come from above ground: streams, lakes, ponds and rivers, and you would need a separate settlement pond to permit large particles to settle out, as well as a sand or gravel filter before the water can be used. The more usual underground sources are wells and boreholes.

There are underground water sources in many places, but establishing a borehole can be extremely expensive; knowing where to drill is a key question, and some consider the centuries'-old practise of dowsing to be a useful and practical skill to detect underground water. Dowsing involves the use of rods or a pendulum, which are said to move in accordance with the proximity to underground water. Explanations for the success of dowsing vary, but one possibility is that the dowser himself is sensitive to underground vibrations, and the rods or pendulum somehow allows these feelings to manifest themselves visibly.

Drinking water from private sources can be contaminated by parasites, protozoa, bacteria and viruses, and the presence of solids, for which reason its use has to be monitored by the local authority. The processes of purification involve some or all of the following: remaining in a settlement tank to allow heavier particles to settle out (for overground water sources), filtration to remove particles (for instance lead, minerals and rust) and direct treatment to kill bacteria and protozoa. Two key devices used are a 'Reverse Osmosis System', whereby natural osmosis separates dissolved substances from water, and ultra-violet sterilization units, which kill bacteria.

If your source of water is limited it could make sense to harvest rainwater for uses such as washing clothes, cars and WC flushing (it's not suitable for drinking). There are systems whereby the leaf debris is filtered out at a collector unit, then fed to an underground tank where it settles, allowing heavy particles to sink and lighter ones to float to the surface. Water is drawn off by way of a floating filter at surface level, from where it is pumped on-demand to supply points – for instance WC cisterns, and the washing machine.

Private Drainage Systems

There are basically two options: a septic tank, which breaks down the sewage before it is released to the environment, and a cesspool, which is emptied at regular intervals. Of the two options, the former is the best in terms of running costs and convenience.

A septic tank has a number of compartmentalized plastic boxes that rely on biological activity to break down the effluent. An electric sewage-treatment plant goes further, aiding the biological process by mechanically aerating and/or vibrating the material. Where you are allowed to release the treated liquid from a septic tank is controlled by the Environment Agency, and their specific requirements change all the time, so you should check their current requirements to find out if your soil conditions are suitable. For discharge from a sewage treatment plant you need to have a 'Consent to Discharge' certificate from the Environment Agency.

In difficult-to-drain soil conditions with high water tables, another method of dispersal of partially treated (by a septic tank) effluent is to pass the discharge through a reed bed filter, which effectively oxygenates the liquid, therefore purifying it. A reed bed filter can be a hole in the ground containing gravel and/or sand or soil, planted with aquatic plants. Foul or partially treated water enters at one end, percolates through the spaces between granules, and exits, purified, at the other. 'Vertical flow' reed beds allow water to flow down from above and drop downwards and out, whereas the less efficient 'horizontal floor' reed beds process the liquid with less help from gravity.

A cesspool is a large underground container, and requires emptying four to six times annually. Both septic tanks and cesspools require emptying of the non-dispersible solid matter (sludge) once or twice annually. Some household chemicals can kill the working bacteria that digest the waste, causing temporary breakdown.

As a way of reducing the money-gulping amount of sewage water, so-called 'grey' water from washbasins, baths, showers and washing machines can sometimes be discharged directly onto the land, providing certain plant-damaging detergents are avoided.

Alternative Heating Fuels

Liquid Petroleum Gas (LPG)
This is similar to natural gas, in that it can power boilers, ranges, cookers and heaters, although these appliances have to be designed or adapted for this fuel. LPG is stored in a large tank rented from the supply company, which has to be sited by them in accordance with the regulations: it must be in the open air, 3m (9ft) away from any boundary or building. This tank is regularly topped up by the company. One of the main supply companies is Flogas UK (www.flogas.co.uk; 0800 574 574). There is a nominal annual charge for hire of the tank, and no installation charges. Disadvantages of LPG are that it is heavier than air and operates at a higher pressure than natural gas, therefore a leak doesn't disperse easily; accordingly safety requirements are very stringent, and leaks are potentially extremely hazardous. All fires have to be fitted with a flame failure safety device.

Oil
This can power central heating boilers and some kitchen ranges or Agas. Fuel oil is stored in a large, plastic tank that has to be installed by a member of Oftec, the Oil-Firing Technical Association (www.oftec.org; 0845 6585080; list of members on the site). Boiler installations have to conform to the building regulations and oil-fired systems usually have to include an automatic shut-off in case of fire.

Electricity Generators

For practical purposes you need to have two generators, one for light load at night-time for fridges and occasional lights, plus the other for normal loads. They run on natural gas or LPG ideally: petrol-run generators are for more industrial uses. Disadvantages are that generators are noisy and require considerable soundproofing, and also need regular servicing and oil-changes. They are also expensive to run.

CHAPTER 3

Building Trade Professionals, Legalities and Finance

PROFESSIONALLY QUALIFIED PEOPLE IN THE CONSTRUCTION INDUSTRY

Surveyor

Services include preparing surveys, plans, schedule of works, costings and valuations. They also conduct Specific Defect Analysis, make sure that work complies with building regulations, undertake project management, do insurance reinstatement and represent clients for litigation purposes.

Members of the Royal Institution of Chartered Surveyors (RICS) residential and building surveying professional groups, offer a range of general and specialist services to homeowners depending on the circumstance. Homeowners or prospective owners should contact a local chartered surveyor to discuss their requirements in full.

The professional body is the Royal Institution of Chartered Surveyors (RICS) (www.rics.org.uk; 0870 333 1600; 'Find a surveyor' service on the website).

Architect

An architect is an expert in design and the optimum use of space. His/her prime role is to advise clients on the most advantageous ways of altering, repairing or extending their building. He defines priorities and limitations, grasps a client's needs and translates these into designs. His design skills equip him to improve on the brief wherever possible. Many architecture practices have websites, and most specialize in a particular field: for instance, a Conservation Architect will deal with old buildings

and be fully conversant with regulations covering Listed Buildings and those in a Conservation Area. A locally based architect is also likely to have knowledge about the local authority's policies and plans. In the UK, a person cannot practise or carry on a business under any name, style or title containing the word 'architect' unless he or she is registered with the Architects' Registration Board (ARB) (*see below*).

Furthermore, architects practising in the UK who are registered with the ARB and are also chartered members of the Royal Institute of British Architects (RIBA) are entitled to describe themselves as 'Chartered Architects' and to use the suffix RIBA after their name; they also maintain their competence to practise through completion of mandatory continuing professional development, and have access to the knowledge base and resources of the RIBA. RIBA publishes a flexible range of Appointment Agreements suitable for use with projects of all sizes and complexity.

Other roles of an architect might include:

1. Investigating the feasibility of the requirements.
2. Developing design proposals.
3. Applying for statutory approvals.
4. Preparing construction information.
5. Obtaining tenders for building work.
6. Administering a building contract.
7. An architect can also arrange other services connected with the project, such as interior design, landscaping or making measured surveys of a site or building.

An extension project at the start of works.

There are a number of professional bodies to which architects belong. First, all architects must legally be registered with The Architects' Registration Board (www.arb.org.uk; 020 7580 5861). In addition to this, they are likely to belong to one or more of the following:

The Royal Institute of British Architects (RIBA)
(www.architecture.com;   www.ribafind.org;   and RIBA Client Services, 020 7307 3700).
   This is the UK charter body for architecture, representing Chartered Architects throughout the UK and overseas. Its mission is to advance archi-

tecture by demonstrating benefit to society and promising excellence in the professions.

The Royal Society of Architects in Wales (RSAW)
(Website as for RIBA; 029 2022 8987)
   Operates within the structural framework of the RIBA in Wales.

The Royal Incorporation of Architects in Scotland (RIAS)
(www.rias.org.uk; 0131 229 7545)
   The professional body for all chartered architects in Scotland.

ABOVE:
**Two-storey
extension,
partially built.**

RIGHT: **Aerated
thermalite
blocks being
used instead of
a conventional
cavity wall
construction.**

Association of Consultant Architects (ACA)
(www.acarchitects.co.uk; 020 8466 9079)

This is the national professional body representing architects in private practice throughout the UK. Founded in 1973, it represents some of the country's leading practices, ranging in size from one-person firms to large, international organizations. It was founded to promote and support UK architectural practices.

ASBA Architects
(www.asba-architects.org; 0800 387310)

Britain's largest network of experienced, independent Chartered Architects specializing in new homes, extensions, conversions and refurbishments. It is a national network of local architects, who specialize in the design of 'one-off' houses and domestic alterations. An ASBA member can offer independent advice from an experienced architect on all aspects of the design and construction of homes, from finding plots to choosing contractors. They can oversee the entire project or just help at the time when you feel you need professional support, and if you employ someone local, they'll have extensive knowledge of the local authorities, buildings and all other relevant local information.

Structural Engineer

Such a person is an expert in how a building is constructed and is the one who diagnoses structural faults and devises strategies to put things right. A structural engineer is consulted if subsidence is suspected or if some part of a building is collapsing or under threat of structural compromise, for whatever reason. This type of engineer selects materials and structures to reinforce or support parts of a building, and is competent to make complex mathematical calculations to ascertain the size and strength of these. The professional body is the Association of Consulting Engineers (ACE) (www.istructe.org; 020 7235 4535). ACE have a directory of member firms, with details of their specialities.

Architectural Technologist

His/her expertise is in technological aspects of construction and design. They can cover many of the roles done by architects and surveyors; for example, surveying, preparing drawings and project management, and if an architectural technologist is fully qualified, they can be in charge of a building project from start to finish. These professionals apply the science of architecture and specialize in the technology of building design and construction. They can lead a building project from inception through to final certification, including managing the coordination of other professionals. Their professional body is the Chartered Institute of Architectural Technologists (CIAT) (www.ciat.org.uk; 020 7278 2206).

Planning Officers, Conservation Officers

Employed by the local authority, Planning Officers for domestic buildings are the people to whom you apply when you want planning permission, which is usually needed for extensions above a certain size. Planning officers for listed buildings (*see below*) are often Conservation Officers (COs) who are familiar with old buildings and frequently are also architects. You need to work with a CO to get Listed Building Consent (LBC) (*see below*) and Planning Permission for alterations/extensions to listed buildings and/or those in a Conservation Area. If your building falls into either of these categories and you want to alter it, always consult a CO at an early stage and try to get them on your side; they'll be able to tell you precisely what is covered by LBC and when it is not needed.

Building Inspector

Building Inspectors work within the Local Authority's Building Control Department, and their job is to make sure that a building conforms to the current building regulations. These apply to all aspects of new extensions, and also to certain jobs, such as renewing/repairing walls or roofs and installing windows, rewiring and so on. If you're having an extension built, you pay a fee for all the site visits at the outset. For anyone physically doing the building work themselves, this is usually very good value for money, because while the Building Inspector has to ensure you do things according to law, in my experience they always offer helpful advice as to how to meet the various regulations, and even give you a great deal of practical building advice. At the completion of the construction of an extension, when the building inspector is satisfied all the work has been done to his satisfaction, he issues you with a 'Certificate of Clearance' stating that it conforms to the current building regulations, and this is vital to have when you sell the house.

LEGALITIES

Party Wall Etc. Act

This Act came into force on 1 July 1997 and applies throughout England and Wales. It provides a framework for presenting and resolving disputes in relation to party walls, boundary walls and excavations near neighbouring buildings. In practice, it mainly applies if your house is semi-detached or terraced, and you wish to drill, alter or otherwise do work on the wall that you share with the neighbour. A party wall is defined as such if it stands astride the boundary of land belonging to two or more different owners. It applies to garden walls, but not fences.

The Act covers various work that is going to be carried out directly to an existing party wall or structure, new building at or astride the boundary line between properties or excavation within 3–6m (10–20ft) of a neighbouring building or structure, depending on the depth of the hole or proposed foundations.

If you intend to do any work to a party wall you must inform all adjoining owners. However, exempted from the Act are such works as drilling into a party wall to fix plugs and screws for ordinary wall units and shelving, cutting into a party wall to add or replace recessed electric wiring and sockets and re-plastering. The point to remember is that the Act is relevant if the planned work might have consequences for the structural strength and support functions of the party wall as a whole, or cause damage to the adjoining owner's side of the wall. Ask a surveyor if you are in doubt.

If the Act applies to a wall you want to work on, first talk to the neighbour, then give notice in writing about what you plan to do. In this note you must put your own name, an address, the address of the building to be worked on, a full description of what you propose to do and when you propose to start. It must be dated and must include a clear statement that it is a notice under the provision of the Act; there is no need to tell the local authority

---

Commonly Used Rights When the Party Wall Etc. Act Applies

- Cutting into a wall to take the bearing of a beam, e.g. for a loft-conversion, or to insert a damp-proof course all the way through the wall.
- To raise the height of the wall and/or increase the thickness of the party wall, and, if necessary, cut off any projections that prevent you from doing so.
- To demolish and rebuild the party wall.
- To underpin the whole thickness of a party wall.
- To protect two adjoining walls by putting a flashing (weatherproofing material) from the higher over the lower, even where this requires cutting into an adjoining owner's independent building.

(LA). You must serve the notice at least two months before starting work. After that time, the adjoining owner may give his/her consent in writing, dissent from the works proposed in writing or do nothing – this should be done within fourteen days. Ideally, sort out any problems face to face. If you cannot get agreement, you then have to agree with the neighbour on appointing an 'Agreed Surveyor' to draw up an award. The 'Agreed Surveyor' should not be the same person you intend to employ, or whom you have already engaged. Alternatively, each owner can appoint a surveyor to draw up the award together. The two appointed surveyors will select a third surveyor if they cannot agree. Usually the building owner who instigated the business has to pay all fees to all surveyors.

Planning Permission

You'll need this if you want to extend, rebuild, convert a house into flats or make a similar change of use, or alter the external appearance of a building. If you extend less than 70m^3, or 15 per cent of the property, you may not need permission, except in some circumstances, but things change all the time, so check with your LA.

Building Control

Most major work has to conform to strict LA (and EEC) building regulations, and the building inspectors who work in this department in the LA charge a (reasonable) fixed fee for their visits. For an extension, as mentioned above, each stage in the project is 'signed off' by the Building Inspector, and at the end a 'Certificate of Clearance', stating that all work has met the required standard is given.

Listed Buildings

If a building is listed it means that it has officially been recognized as being of architectural or historical importance, and listing adds around 5 per cent to its value. Drawbacks, however, are that ordinary routine repair jobs involve bureaucracy and meetings, discussions and the preparation of plans, in order to get Listed Building Consent for the work. A conundrum of the rules means that any change made before the listing date cannot be removed or altered without permission, even if this is the removal of something added in the 1970s. Breaking the rules can blight a future sale or even lead to fines and imprisonment.

English Heritage in England and CADW in Wales classify buildings according to their importance. Practically this means that mainly stately homes and publicly owned structures are either

Grade I or Grade II*, which is 6 per cent of the total. Grade Is are 'of exceptional importance, consequently rigorously protected', while Grade II*s are 'of particular importance and perhaps contain outstanding features', or 'of more than special interest'. The majority of listed buildings are Grade IIs, defined as 'of special interest, which warrant every effort being made to preserve them'. Almost all pre-eighteenth-century buildings are listed, most between 1700 and 1840, but with only the most notable examples after 1840. Historic Scotland divides its listed buildings into categories A, B and C, referring, respectively, to them being of national, regional and local importance.

Listed Building Consent

Listed Building Consent (LBC) is required for altering a listed building in any way, inside or outside, unless you're doing repairs with like-for-like materials. However, a repair that involves the use of even slightly different materials constitutes an alteration, so it is important to check before starting with your local CO. LBC is also needed for 'Demolition of any part and of any works (external or internal) affecting its character or appearance'. For Grade II buildings LBC is granted by the Conservation Officer (CO) of the local authority, while Grade I and II*s additionally need sanction from English Heritage (EH). In addition, work has to comply with Local Authority Building Regulations, and for an addition or alteration, standard Planning Permission will also be required.

Conservation Areas (CAs)

These are designated by local authorities to be 'any areas of special architectural or historic interest, that the character of which it is desirable to preserve or enhance'. Factors considered include buildings, layout of roads, general appearance and features of special historic or architectural interest. CAs should clearly identify what it is about an area that should be preserved or enhanced. External work on an unlisted building that's in a Conservation Area requires permission from the local authority.

CAs can be historic town or village centres, eighteenth- and nineteenth-century residential suburbs, model housing estates or even lengths of canal. 'Enhancement' means reinforcement of the qualities that warranted the designation, and takes the form of sympathetic development of sites or 'Positive Proposals', e.g. restoring architectural features. 'Special attention' means the council have particular controls over what happens within a CA, while 'Special Interest' is the special architectural or historic interest that justifies designation. Un-listed buildings within a CA do not qualify for VAT relief.

HOW DO YOU FIND A BUILDER?

As with most things, the best way to find a trustworthy and reliable builder is by personal recommendation from someone you trust. However, even this is not a foolproof method, since the type of job done for the person making the recommendations may be totally different to yours, making their good experience of no relevance to you. If you can't get a recommendation from a friend, neighbour or relative who has had the same sort of project as you have in mind, try a trade association, as they can recommend local members to come and quote for your project. You can get further advice on finding a builder from the Federation of Master Builders' (FMB) website: it is the largest trade association in the UK construction industry. FMB members have to pass its membership criteria, which includes an inspection of a job in progress, having liability (and employer, if necessary) insurance and other financial checks.

Always avoid the person who solicits work by knocking on your door: this is a sure sign that he's short of work. Again, you can get more advice on this from the FMB through its 'Nail the Rogues' campaign (www.nailtherogues.org.uk). Also remember that while you may distrust an unknown builder, they may distrust you: many builders have experienced unscrupulous clients, who either refuse to pay or pay only a proportion of what was agreed. The programmes about cowboy builders on television are horrifying and serve to illustrate that, more often than not, if you are swindled by a crooked builder, there is not much practical redress according to law if you don't have a legally binding contract – and even if you do, it may not be financially viable to take legal action. However, crooked builders are the exception, the vast majority are reasonable and fair, and want to keep their reputation and encourage recommendations.

Conservation Areas

Key Facts
- If the building is unlisted, only the outside is controlled and the inside is exempt.
- Any proposals for change are subject to harder tests.
- There may be an increase in statuary control on alterations to the fabric of the property and work on trees: six weeks' notice is required for cutting down or lopping trees.
- There are restrictions on new development.
- Grants for repair and maintenance might be on offer from the local authority or English Heritage.
- Boundaries can be changed and a CA can be cancelled.

Practicalities
- 'Permitted development', meaning certain kinds of development that are allowed outside a CA without planning permission, e.g. an extension under a certain size, is not allowed within a CA.
- You need planning permission for external features such as cladding and dormer windows.
- LAs can also stipulate where you can change windows, doors and roofs, and you may not be allowed to take down a boundary wall to allow front-garden parking.
- Demolition, wholly or partly, has to have permission.
- Development of a property just outside a CA will need the protected area to be taken into consideration when planning permission is sought.

Expert Quote

Architect Roger Mears, of Roger Mears Architects:

The first principle of all historic building practice is to retain and conserve what you can of existing fabric. Completely renewing damaged fabric, however accurately, can be no substitute for retaining the qualities and patina of original materials. For example, old joinery (windows, doors, panelling, etc.) was made by hand with a multitude of different profiles and methods of construction, so in repairing it you are saving the hand-craftsmanship and adding your own contribution to the layers of history. The timber used, particularly softwoods, is generally of superior quality to anything obtainable today. The avoidance of sapwood and the close grain and high resin content of the first-growth trees used in the past means that the durability of old joinery is almost un-matchable today – just think how long it has lasted to date (hundreds of years?) and compare it with the short life of modern joinery, whether of timber, plastic or metal, which often needs replacing after thirty to sixty years.

Builders' Trade Associations

In the UK, anyone can operate as a builder and there is no obligation to register a company officially, or apply to have a licence. However, many builders choose to join trade associations, such as the Federation of Master Builders, or the National Federation of Builders (NFB). Members usually have to pass membership criteria to join these organizations but it is worth checking exactly what the organizations do to 'vet' their members, as each organization is different. Some bodies, such as the FMB, NFB and the government-backed scheme TrustMark, also allow their members to offer warranties on the work they do. If you would like to purchase a warranty, be explicit and do not assume it is included. These organizations tend to run 'Find a Builder' services too. Some trade associations offer a complaints process, should there be any cause for complaint during your project.

But take heed of Dominic Littlewood's *Cowboy Builders* (Channel 5, TV) warning, that if a builder claims to be a member of a reputable organization, check with the organization that he or his company is still a current member, not a lapsed one or claiming membership falsely: remember, anyone can print a business card or letterhead

FMB builder on site. Federation of Master Builders

claiming membership of an organization, so it's always vital to check.

The Leading Building Trade Associations
The Federation of Master Builders (www.fmb.org.uk; 020 7242 7583) is the largest trade association in the construction industry and operates a 'Find a Builder' service on its website, and also offers free contracts.

National Federation of Builders (www.builders.org.uk; 0845 057 8160) is a modern, proactive organization that has built up a reputation for sound judgement. It provides vital resources in key areas for builders' contractors and house builders across England and Wales. 'Find a builder' service on the website, as well as useful tips on finding a builder.

TrustMark (www.trustmark.org.uk; 01344 630804) is a not-for-profit organization, licensed by government and supported by consumer protection groups. 'Find a tradesmen' service on the website, as well as much useful information.

Getting Tenders from Builders

Ask three suitable builders to give you a quote for your project. Give them your own written brief or specification (as written by a surveyor or architect). Each builder should then give you a quotation, estimate or a mixture of the two. A quotation is binding and sets out the full project details and cost from the outset. An estimate is merely that: it may change. Therefore, it is recommended you ask for a quote in order to avoid any nasty surprises at the end of your project. A quotation is ideal but not always possible, e.g. in a situation where it is only possible to discover the extent of repair work needed by dismantling a floor or other part of the building – or indeed there may be decay or rot that is concealed behind or underneath something.

A builder may produce his own specification or mark prices on yours (which ought to include a description of work and materials). When deciding which person to choose, there are a number of important factors to bear in mind: cost, and who you instinctively like best, can trust and feel you can

work with well. What did previous clients say and what did you think of the workmanship in previous clients' homes?

Formal Standard Contracts

Some contracts, which are often used for small jobs in England and Wales, are the JCT Minor Works Building Contract and the JCT suite of Building Contracts for a homeowner/occupier, some of which are intended for those who don't use an architect or surveyor and wish to deal directly with the builder. These are long, very detailed and complicated documents, their purpose being to

How aerated CMU blocks are bonded against a brick frontage.

Block wall being constructed from the foundations up (trench blocks and bricks used below ground).

pin down every aspect of the job at the outset and for fair retribution if one side is at fault, hopefully without the need for litigation. Principally the contract is a questionnaire with blank spaces. The kinds of issues that may be covered in a contract include:

- Description of work to be done.
- What statutory approvals the customer will obtain (meaning planning permission/building regulation approval).
- What facilities the contractor is allowed to use on site free of charge (e.g. toilet/bathroom use).
- The price.
- Stage payments, if any.
- How long the work will last.
- Contractual insurances.
- What hours the contractor is permitted to do the work.
- Whether the premises will be occupied during this work.
- How disputes are to be handled.

Other Contracts

This can be a formal contract between you and a chartered surveyor, or the free contract you can download from the FMB website. Alternatively, it can simply be a Letter of Agreement between you

The trench blocks and brickwork up to ground level.

Five Top Tips for Finding a Good Builder
(The following is the copyright of the Federation of Master Builders.)

1. Be specific and prepare a detailed brief. Be as clear as you can about what you want, as this can make a huge difference to quotes.
2. Choose a reputable builder. Ask friends and family for recommendations or check with a trade association, such as the FMB and its Find a Builder website. Don't be afraid to ask for references and speak to previous clients about their experience of the builder: did they finish the project on time and within budget? Another thing to consider is, does the trader have a landline telephone number, rather than just a mobile number?
3. Get at least three quotes, which should include the whole project, including materials, removal of rubbish and making good after the project has finished. When you are ready to decide, don't just go with the cheapest, consider communication and quality of workmanship too.
4. Use a contract. You can download a free contract to use with any builder from the FMB website.
5. Never pay the full cost of the project upfront. Agree a payment plan as part of the contract. Using a credit card to pay may offer you more protection.

Stages to Completion

1. Evaluate what you have. For a newly acquired property, the surveyor's structural report will itemize defects. Be sure you have accurate, measured, drawings.
2. Sort out your finances. Work out how much money you can spare and, if needed, arrange a mortgage, remortgage or loan.
3. List the jobs. Always include the ones that are vital and desirable, prioritizing the vital. The budget determines how many of the 'desirable' jobs can be done.
4. Building regulations and planning permission. Building regulations ensure that homes are safe, healthy and energy efficient. You could contact your local Building Control Department before any work begins to make sure it will meet the relevant building regulations. Planning Permission and Party Wall Agreements may also be needed, but your local Building Control Department will be able to advise you on this too.
5. Get tenders from builders or other trades people. Then choose one and arrange for them to start.
6. The actual build.
7. Assess things at the end. Make sure that all is satisfactory on completion.

---

and the surveyor or you and the builder. Using a Letter of Agreement makes sense for small projects.

Paying the Builder

It is not advisable to pay large sums of money at the start of the project, although builders may ask for a deposit before the project starts. Payment terms should be set out in the contract you use. You should ensure you pay each instalment promptly. Retain a 'defective work percentage' (up to 10 per cent) until finishing touches (snagging) are complete.

Tips

DO
- Put everything in writing before work starts and make sure any changes are agreed and written down along with any extra costs.
- Plan ahead and do not rush things.
- Examine all possibilities, then decide what you want at the beginning and stick to this aim.
- Have a clear definitive idea of precisely what you want at the outset and then stick to this.
- Inform your home insurance company of work to be done.
- Choose an established builder if you can, ideally after a recommendation.
- Make sure your builder is covered by public liability insurance; it is worth noting that all FMB members must have this as a condition of membership.
- In the Contract or Letter of Agreement stipulate your wishes as to use of your toilet, kitchen facilities, whether smoking is permitted on-site and working hours.
- Check all references.

DO NOT
- Change your mind about any aspects of the job, unless you are prepared to pay extra.
- Pay for the whole project or large parts of it up front; a deposit or some materials cost may be paid initially, but use your common sense on how much to hand over before work begins.
- Expect verbal agreements to be of any use.
- Choose the cheapest builder without carefully checking the details on his agreed specification.

Case History 1

Alison M bought a large house that needed a lot of alterations and repairs, in a completely strange area. Friends recommended a local company, the quote seemed fine, so she arranged for them to start work. She didn't do a contract or write a Letter of Agreement because it didn't seem worth it, as the builder was friendly and he had been recommended. Her husband was working away at the time so she had to deal with all the contact with the builder.

I had walls taken down and put up and had a bathroom installed, basically reorganizing and re-jigging the space, so it was more what we wanted. The builder was a nightmare. The first week was fine, then his men would come in at 8 or 9am for a few hours on a Monday then disappear, usually not coming back until the end of the week. They always appeared on a Friday, though, because I paid them on a weekly basis. Every week he'd give me reasons why things hadn't been done and would tell me that he couldn't continue the following week unless I gave him money so he could pay his men.

It should have taken three weeks, but it took three months! They never ever cleaned up after themselves, there was rubble everywhere, even in the bedrooms. At the end he tried to charge more money than was agreed, but I refused. In fact, I stopped the last cheque payment because he'd just gone away without finding me a plumber to fix the leak he'd caused. I'd had a tiler who'd never done tiling before, and he had to take all the tiles off and do them again because they weren't straight! They plastered a ceiling and never even removed a ceiling-fitting lampshade, just plastered up to its edge! Finally when they'd left for the day and had supposedly finished, I saw water on the wallpaper on the landing – a plumbing leak.

A friend came round and told me about 'snagging' – where you detail all the un-finished jobs before giving the builder his final payment. He helped me compose two full A4 pages of problems and snags. I told the builder I wasn't paying until he fixed the things on the list. He became really unpleasant, an absolute bully, until my husband came round and suddenly his attitude miraculously altered entirely. It wasn't all a disaster – in fact the guys he employed were actually very nice, and there was an agreeable atmosphere in the house while they were working – mind you I'd go in the kitchen for coffee and find they were all eating sandwiches and watching my television without even asking! The main feeling I had was that my space was completely invaded. The worst thing

---

Expert Quote

Brian Berry, Director of External Affairs at the FMB:

Finding a builder you can rely on needn't be difficult provided you take some basic steps. First, try and be as specific as you can about what work you want done, and set this out in a brief, as this can make a huge difference to quotes. When you have done this you can then start looking for a builder. The best way to find a quality reliable builder is to ask friends, family and neighbours for recommendations. If you don't get any suitable recommendations, check with a trade association such as the FMB. Once you have a few builders in mind, ask three to come and visit the project site, provide them with your brief, and have a chat with them about what you are hoping to achieve. Ask them to give you a quote for the whole project including materials, removal of rubbish and making good after the project has finished. Also ask for references from previous clients and ask to go and see the projects to get an idea of their workmanship. Ask the previous clients about their experience of the builder. For example, did the builder finish the project on time and within budget? When you are ready to decide, don't just go with the cheapest, consider other factors such as how well you communicate with the builder and the quality of their workmanship. When you have selected the builder you want, make sure you use a contract. You can download a free contract to use with any builder from the FMB website. Finally, never pay the full cost of the project upfront and agree a payment plan as a part of the contract.

was never knowing who was going to turn up. One day I came home and the door was left open and my dog was running in the road! I rang the builder and I was screaming. He almost patted me on the head, he was arrogant and patronizing. But next time I saw him, I stuck to my guns – showed him the snagging list and said when he'd done the jobs I'd pay half what I owed, then withhold the rest for another month, to make sure nothing else cropped up.

If I ever do it again would I do things differently? Yes I certainly would.

Case History 2

Tim Lowe's experiences:

I bought Great House, an early eighteenth-century merchant's house in West Wales, in 1998. It was my first 'restoration' project and I soon realized that my enthusiasm far outstripped my knowledge and ability. The project has ultimately taken some fifteen years and as my learning increased, I came to understand the difference between 'repair' and 'careful conservation', as opposed to 'speculative restoration'.

One of the first things I did was attend a course run by the Society for the Protection of Ancient Buildings (SPAB), specifically for homeowners. It was a salutary experience, which taught me to respect the work of those that have gone before. The investment of the original artisans and the imprint that they have left on the fabric of your building is precious, and it is irreplaceable once lost. Generally, by following the route that those builders took, one can work through most of the problems that an old building throws up and one should always try to replace as little as possible, as almost everything is repairable if you are prepared to take your time. A rough stone floor, for example, if conservatively repaired and repointed, can look a million dollars, as can most of the unique features in your house.

Whether your house was built in 1570 or 1970, the loss of original features, however seemingly small and insignificant, denude your building of the very character that made you want it in the first place.... So hang on to each and every one of them. As an example, an old toilet that has done service for thirty years can, with a little care and

attention, accent your modern bathroom design and complement the limestone freestanding bath that you've always promised yourself in a way that a modern equivalent never can. Similarly, original fitted cupboards and shelving, properly repaired and painted, will enhance, not detract from, your ambition to create a contemporary look. In summary, old looks great alongside modern and there is actually no inherent conflict there.

An architect once said to me, 'Let the building tell you what it is capable of and don't try to get too much out of it, or you'll spoil it.' He was absolutely right. If you approach a building with respect for its original capabilities and don't try to turn it into something that it isn't, you are on the right track. All you should be aiming to do is add your layer of history to those that are already inherent in the fabric of the building.

In short, my advice, having made many more mistakes than I care to remember, is to take the time to really think about what you want to achieve and then to question your core assumptions before proceeding.... Ask yourself whether you really need to maximize the available space by converting the old stable block and, even if you do, how about incorporating the old loose boxes and other equine features into the rooms that you're planning? I've seen it done and it looks great.

Similarly, when your contractor tells you he's found the old well (there normally is one), think about taking the time to dig it out, put a grate or some glass over it and then try lighting it. I've done this in Great House and I feel it showcases a major part of my building's story.

If it's your first project and there are planning issues involved, you'll need to choose an architect and make sure they have sympathy for your kind of project. Shop around and find previous examples of their work – most have illustrated portfolios on their websites – to check whether they complement your vision. If you don't need an architect and your project is just about repair and updating services, be careful to choose a professional contractor who actually cares about fabric (those that don't care make themselves fairly obvious from the start) and don't let anyone tell you that there is only one way to do a job. This is a classic tactic and can be very intimidating when uttered by a seemingly experienced expert, but there is always a second opinion and you should keep asking people until you find someone who shows real sincerity of purpose and feeling for the building. The bottom line is that everything is repairable and problems can always be worked around.

If you've already completed your first project and have accumulated some experience, the real fun is in building your own team of sensitive craftspeople and managing the new project slowly but steadily through each stage. Repairing old buildings is an endlessly fascinating pursuit, which gives me unparalleled pleasure. Fifteen years on, I'm now on my fourth repair project and I still learn something new every day.

GETTING MONEY/ INSURANCE ISSUES

Grants

These days getting a grant is a bleak prospect, as practically all these come from cash-strapped LAs. There are Local Authority House Renovation Grants, which are generally designed to bring houses up to an acceptable modern standard of hygiene and safety, and are only relevant if the property is badly neglected, and are generally for essential amenities, such as toilets and bathrooms. Otherwise the LA can give you help to 'adapt improve or repair your home' at their discretion. It has of course to be your home. There are also Home Energy Efficiency schemes that give grants. One of the leading ones is Warm Front (England) and Nest (Wales). Also you may get help with insulating your home.

For a listed building, there are, rarely, possibilities for getting grants in certain situations. English Heritage might consider a grant for a building at risk, but only if it is a Grade I or II*. There are Local Authority Historic Building Grants, but these are extraordinarily rare, as councils have very little spare cash. Historic Scotland also has similar schemes, as does CADW for Wales.

Expert Quote

Beverley Winterhalter, of RJW Associates, gives the following advice on finding finance:

With any project, the key to success is organizing your finances at the outset to ensure that you have the money you need as the project progresses. Finding the right mortgage for a self-build project is crucial to ensuring its success. A mortgage for a self-build project differs from a residential mortgage; with a self-build mortgage the money is released in stages as the build progresses. There are, however, different ways in which this money can be released, depending on the product choice that fits your circumstances. When you are renovating or converting you are likely to need money for the initial purchase of the property and then for the building works. Some mortgage lenders will refuse to lend on properties that are uninhabitable, while others will be based on the current value of the house, but will then not lend anything further until the project is complete and the property can be revalued. This is known as applying a retention to the borrowing and will only be suitable if you have access to sufficient cash to pay for all of the building work. An alternative is a stage-payment mortgage, where the building work is broken down into identifiable stages, normally at the end of each build stage, known as arrears. With a traditional arrears stage-payment mortgage the lender will release money to buy the property, usually up to 75 per cent of the purchase price or value of the property and will then release the money for the building costs with each stage payment being made at the end of each stage, i.e. in arrears of the work being done. This type of mortgage may be suitable if you have access to cash to pay for the deposit on the property and the early stages of the building work. With so many different options for financing a project it is important to speak to an expert to discuss your plans as early as possible.

Mortgages

For a dilapidated building with a low value, there are some lenders who specialize in 'staged releases' of money as work progresses, each tranche triggered by the lender's stage-by-stage assessment of the increasing value of the building. This means you won't waste interest payments or have cash unused until it's actually needed. This is helpful in a situation where you need to borrow most of the purchase price plus the cash for the renovation, but initially there may not be enough equity in the dilapidated building to set up a mortgage at all. The company's valuer judges your detailed plans and gives a 'when finished' second valuation, which is what is used to broker a deal.

Insurance When Having Building Work Done to Your House

Checklist
- Have liability cover for anyone you employ on the site, because if they have an accident, you could be sued.
- Clarify the insurance position with your contractor, as his insurance should cover the building while he's doing major structural work.
- Don't insure in joint names between you and the contractor – a contractor's claim due to his negligence could result in both companies refusing to pay.
- Give your insurer exact details of what work is being done.
- Generally, discuss what's being done with your house insurer and take their advice.

CHAPTER 4

How a House is Built

FOUNDATIONS

A foundation for a wall, sometimes called 'footings', is made by excavating a trench into which concrete or special concrete 'trench' blocks are put, so as to provide a solid base onto which you can build a wall. These footings follow the lines of the proposed walls, and within this area – the eventual ground floor of the building – the soil is removed to a lesser depth than the footings, prior to the laying of flooring material. In medieval times, a timber 'cill' beam was laid directly into the earth onto which the timber frame was erected, and this rotted quite quickly. Many Georgian and Victorian foundations were very shallow by today's standards, merely a shallow trench into which bricks were laid.

ABOVE: **Concrete being delivered into a foundation trench via a chute.** Julian Owen Associates Architects

TOP RIGHT: **A foundation trench for the footings.** Julian Owen Associates Architects

BOTTOM RIGHT: **Foundation block work on a large construction site.** Julian Owen Associates Architects

Foundation trench for footings for extension.

Concrete filling the bottom part of foundation trench, as a base for the block work.

The top layer of soil is called 'vegetable' or 'top' soil, varying from 25mm (1in) to 300mm (12in) in depth, so it is usual for the depth of foundation to at least go down to well below this depth, since this loose soil would not support the weight of a building without compacting. Underneath this is the 'subsoil', which is normally robust enough to build onto. The density of the soil, whether it's of clay, chalk, sand or gravel, varies considerably, and for any modern building your local authority has strict guidelines as to the depth you need to go, dependent on local conditions.

It is, and always has been, usual to have foundations that are wider than the wall, so as to spread the load on the subsoil. This was effected by laying several brick 'footing' courses, alternatively laying a strip of concrete, both of these being wider than the wall. The ground floor is normally designed so that its final top surface is at least 15cm (6in) above ground level, as a protection against dampness rising from the ground soil.

Pre-stressed concrete lintels for use in foundation work, to bridge a sewer pipe below ground.

WALLS

Timber-Framed Houses

These were basically a wooden framework of large timbers. The spaces so formed between the timbers had horizontal and vertical wooden staves (wattle) wedged between them, over which 'daub' (a mixture of mud, sand, straw, cow manure and water) was applied to both sides, progressively filling these panels. When dry, this material was compatible with the surrounding large timbers in that it could flex and move in the same way. Later on it became fashionable to remove the wattle and daub infill, and replace it with brickwork.

Brick

(*See* Chapter 9).

Originally, brick walls were solid, without a cavity, with various types of brick 'bond' that

A medieval building being renovated.

The beauty of bricklaying.

created a robust solid structure, the idea always being that row upon row, the joins were to be staggered, so as not to allow a line of weakness. More modern alternatives to bricks are concrete masonry units (CMUs), also known as breeze blocks, for the internal leaf of a cavity wall or a single non-cavity wall made of large 'aerated' CMUs, which are full of air-entraining holes, thus removing the need for a cavity at all. Early mortars to bond the stone blocks or bricks together were of sand and lime, and were relatively soft. The invention of cement permitted mortars (and renders) that set rock hard.

Cavity Walls
(*See* Chapter 5).

During the 1850s, the concept was invented of two half-brick thick walls built one in front of the other, separated by a cavity, with regular stiffening devices (ties) installed to connect them, so as to create a rigid unified structure. The principle of weight distribution is that the inner leaf of the wall carries all floor and roof loads, leaving the outer leaf as a weatherproof skin. In heavy rain, water can completely penetrate the outer leaf, and the idea is for water to drain away down the cavity without impinging on the inner leaf. In structural terms, the wall ties also lend support to the internal, load-bearing leaf of wall. Thus

solidity and weatherproofing qualities were addressed, unless the ties acted as a waterproof bridge across the two: this could happen if the ties caught mortar 'dabs' from above during construction, which remain inside the wall acting as a water conduit.

The 1875 Building Act advocated use of waterproofed iron ties in ventilated cavities. By the 1920s wall-tie construction was regularized in standards and codes. The importance of the ties and their resistance to corrosion was crucial. Outer leafs of walls would get soaked, and the end of bare iron ties would corrode. Galvanized mild steel had improved resistance to corrosion, but unfortunately these galvanized coatings themselves could break down.

Stone
(*See* Chapter 9).

Stone construction was either regular, where similarly sized blocks were laid in courses, or irregular, where a mass of random-sized stone, cobbles or knapped flint were held together by a lime mortar, giving a face of stonework on both sides. Stone-faced walling means covering inferior stone or brickwork with attractive thin slabs of stone, typically ashlar. Corner stones (quoins) were often cut decoratively to create a feature, predominantly for Georgian houses.

A lovely medieval stone-and-flint built building.

Flint walls are either of rounded stones that stand proud of the background (cobbled work) or show a 'knapped' surface – each flint split to show glossy blackness. They are either laid in courses the full thickness of wall (200–355mm/8–14in) or built as facings against stone or brick buildings. The old method was to build up a mixture of flint stones and mortar between two wooden shuttering boards that were afterwards removed. Incorporated in flint walls were quoins and rows of bricks or stone beside window and door openings, as well as at the wall's base, and these are known as 'dressings'. Styles of flint construction are:

- Square knapped. Flints are knapped (split) to give a flat square face and uniform height and thin mortar beds.
- Random knapped. The flint stones are knapped to a flat face but are of random size with no regular courses and variations of colour.
- Random semi-knapped. Random knapped with natural stones set in.

- Coursed work. Knapped to a precise height to match the accompanying brick courses with a mix of knapped and natural faces.
- Cobble work/pebbles. Unknapped pebbles laid in courses with deeply recessed joints to expose rounded faces.
- Galleting. When small pieces of flint (gallets) are pushed into mortar joints.

Openings in Walls

Windows and door openings require a beam across the top extending beyond the opening to support the wall area above, and these supports are called lintels. In the past, timber was used, which can frequently rot inside the wall. More recently, concrete lintels superseded timber and still are used, the concrete lintels having steel rods cast in them to facilitate the required tensile strength. Lightweight metal lintels are now used, many made by the company 'Catnic' and these are relatively light box-metal constructions, cleverly designed to support considerable weights and also provide the correct type of insulation.

Finishes

Brick walls are either left natural or covered in render, which is a mixture of binder (cement or previously lime) and sand, to give a continuous surface, or pebble-dashed to create an attractive pebbly finish. Internally, brick walls are plastered.

FLOORS AND CEILINGS

Early ground floors were merely flagstones laid onto the earth, then timber floors were formed, originally as a 'suspended timber floor', whereby timber joists were laid at regular intervals, supported by

---

Landmarks in Wall Building

Medieval period: timber-frame construction, featuring close-studding, meaning that the gaps between the timbers were the same width as the timbers themselves.

1500 onwards: pargetting (lime- and gypsum-based plaster mixes) was used for covering exterior walls, and similar materials used to cover internal walls.

1550: thin, handmade bricks were in vogue. Timber was in shorter supply, meaning that the panels in timber-framed buildings enlarged.

1550–1620: oak was used for building most houses. Handmade bricks were not of uniform thickness, and required thick mortar beds to unify the rows.

1550–1650: lime mortars were more freely available, and heavy roofs could rest along the full length of an unsupported brick wall, so that timber frames were not now needed.

1550–1784: bricks increased in thickness progressively, finally reaching today's 75mm (3in) thickness.

1560–1610: brick buildings were built in the south east, spreading to rest of the country. Brick infilling was used in timber-framed structures, replacing wattle-and-daub.

1560–1720: English brick bond was most popular.

1500 to early 1700s: red brick was the most common brick.

16th century: flint was often used, often rendered over.

Late 1500s: brick building predominated in the south, whereas stone construction was common in areas where it was quarried. Town houses were mostly timber framed.

1666: the Great Fire of London that destroyed so many timber buildings, made brick more popular.

1700: Flemish brick bond began to replace English brick bond.

Early 18th century: windows and doors in brick frontages were emphasized, using a stone of contrasting colour. Quoins (corner stones) were incorporated into buildings as a feature.

1700s: the use of grey, brown and yellow bricks was becoming more widespread. Ashlar blocks were chosen for quoins. Stucco was much in evidence.

1700s to 1800s: mathematical tiles were used to conceal walls. Flintwork was now considered decorative and was not concealed with render.

1769: Coade stone was first produced, then used until around 1900.

1784: a brick tax was introduced, meaning that stone was used more. Stucco often concealed brick facades, and mathematical tiles were used to mimic bricks.

Late-18th century: wattle-and-daub construction ended.

1800–1837: stucco was very popular, as was false ashlaring.

1838: William Aspdin invented Ordinary Portland Cement, which subsequently began to replace lime as binder in mortars and renders.

1850: damp-proof courses were invented, meaning that walls didn't have to dry from the inside.

1850s on: proliferation of the railways, meaning stone and brick could be transported anywhere, so building was no longer restricted to vernacular stone and brick. Bricks mainly machine made, of regular size, therefore thinner mortar courses used. Cavity walls were invented.

1850–1900: yellow bricks were less fashionable in London, and mainly used for working class homes.

1851: the brick tax was repealed.

1852 onwards: cement was superseding lime as a binder for mortars and renders.

1900: cement was in general use, and lime was practically obsolete.

1980s: lime was rediscovered, initially for the repair of lime-mortared buildings, latterly to be used in some new-builds.

LEFT: **Ceiling joists laid onto block work prior to the flat roof being built above.**

BELOW: **Impressive timber pitched-roof structure being built.**
Julian Owen Associates Architects

brickwork at each end, and had floorboards nailed onto them. The ends of the timber joists were set into the wall at each end, and if waterproofing was not considered, these joist ends can frequently rot. A concrete floor is laid on hardcore on earth, and nowadays will incorporate one or more damp-proofing membranes. On top of the concrete is a layer of 50mm (2in) of sand and cement, called screed, which gives an ultra-smooth surface.

Upper floors were, and are still, usually timber joists set into the walls, with floorboards nailed on top. Modern building practices allow for separa-

Pitched roof structure being built. Julian Owen Associates Architects

tion of timber and masonry, e.g. 'hanging' the joists from metal joist hangers, brackets that are set into mortar joints, and which offer a 'cradle' on which the timber rests.

The joist undersides are used as a base on which to build the ceiling for the room below. In the past, small timber laths would be nailed to the joists, then plaster layers applied onto this, pressed hard so that plaster oozed between the laths to lock it in place, then a second top coat of plaster applied, known as a lath-and-plaster ceiling. Nowadays plasterboard is normally nailed directly to the joists, and a layer of plaster applied to its surface.

Modern Timber Flooring

It is very common now to fit wooden floors on top of existing floorboards – if the floor is not nailed to the subfloor, this type is termed a 'floating' floor, whereas if the timbers are nailed down, it is called a 'fixed' floor. Modern timber flooring used in this way is described as 'engineered', meaning that the planks are designed to lock together permanently so that the joins are invisible. Solid, hardwood floors are the most expensive and attractive option, and might be used to replace floorboards, or more likely nailed on top of them. 'Multi-layer' wooden floors are made of a layer of hardwood bonded to a sandwich of softwood boards, and it's the latter that has the profiled engineered edges. 'Laminates' are made either from layers of paper impregnated with resins, or by bonding a plastic laminate with a wood pattern to a base; this is then bonded to fibreboard.

PITCHED ROOFS

The earliest type of roof was called a cruck and was made from twin pairs of trees lashed together, and there was no difference between the continuously curving walls and the roof. From this evolved the standard house with upright walls and a pitched roof. The pitched roof is a separate unit, timber framework supporting rows of timber battens on which tiles or slates are fixed. The angle of pitch corresponds to the roofing surface materials' water permeability, meaning slate or tile roofs have a much shallower pitch than thatch. A simple gabled roof has a plain triangular wall at each end, and a hipped roof has four sloping planes meeting at a ridge, which is shorter than the building's length. In a mansard roof, each of the four roof slopes splits into two angled planes, thereby creating more loft space.

The Pitched Roof's Timber Framework
(See Glossary)

A timber framework (visible in the roof space) is covered by slates, tiles or thatch. The main beams of a pitched roof meet at an angle at the house's apex (the ridge) forming an inverted V shape, with their bases resting on walls. Because the roof's weight tends to splay these timbers apart, they are braced together at the bottom with 'ties' or 'tie beams', or higher up with 'collars' or 'collar beams' (thus forming an A shape), and sometimes ties and collars are used. Also, additional struts can be used to support the structure at other points, usually linking these to party walls.

The most common type is called 'double roof' construction, where the principal rafters and the small common rafters have lengthways purlins sandwiched between them. In hipped roofs, the purlins are usually mitre-joined at the corners, forming a continuous band around the house. In a mansard roof, the roof slopes front and back are divided into two by means of struts and rafters, which surround a central rectangular area, thereby forming a large central void.

Roof Coverings
Tiles and slates are described in detail in Materials (see Chapter 9).

The interior of a newly built pitched roof space.

RIGHT: **Newly laid slate roofs, meeting at a valley.** GWS Roofing Specialists Ltd

BELOW: **Huge roof being laid with roofing tiles.** Clarke Roofing

Very large, flat roof, newly constructed.
Breyer Group PLC

either hooked or tied to the rafters. Straw top-coats are fixed by means of closely spaced spars driven into the basecoat. Progressive layers cover the fixings of the courses below, apart from the final top-course, which is covered by the ridge. The main panels are called 'case work', as opposed to the ridge area. The straw bales are fixed to the roof and previous thatch layers using hazelwood pieces.

Once complete, long-straw roofs are raked down, whereas combed wheat-reed thatchwork must be sheared to an even surface finish before the eaves are trimmed. The ridge area is done separately, and Norfolk reed thatch sedge is sometimes used for this. This part is sometimes trimmed to fancy shapes, e.g. points and scallops.

FLAT ROOFS

This type of roofing is common for single-storey extensions, as well as for small sections of roofing, often subliminal to a larger pitched roof. It is also used in a roofing situation where space does not allow for a pitched roof. Although called flat, there has to be a minimal slope, of at least 1 in 80.

The usual structure is comprised of an area of timber, flat panels or planks, onto which layers of roofing felt are bonded, to effect a waterproof seal. Problem points are usually at edges and

Thatch
Norfolk (water) reed, combed wheat reed and long straw are the principal materials used for thatching. These are arranged in thick, parallel, overlapping layers, pointing down the roof slope. The roof's pitch has to be 45 degrees, with a large overhang.

The thatch is laid in horizontal courses or vertical strips called lanes or stulches. When fitted to a bare roof-frame, as opposed to on top of previous thatch, the material is held by means of 'sways',

The final capsheet being laid over a roof and the parapet for a single-storey flat roof.

corners. Prior to the invention of roofing felt, layers of lead, zinc or copper were used. Since the early 1900s these felts were made from rag, wood fibre or asbestos, materials that had a limited life and are now superseded by more efficient felts made with improved bitumen materials and their composition is polyester-based. These new materials are known as reinforced bitumen membranes (RBM). Concrete is often used to make flat roofs in blocks of flats and was also used for some pre-war houses.

How a Flat Roof is Made

The plywood or oriented strand board (OSB) panels or timber boards are referred to as 'roof decking', and are supported by timber joists laid on edge, with the ceiling plasterboard fixed to the underneath of the latter; nailed on top of the joists are tapering timbers, called 'firring', to give the necessary slight slope for the surface. Insulation panels are fitted either above the decking or sandwiched between the joists above the ceiling plasterboard. If the insulation is fitted on top of the roof decking, the structure is termed a 'warm roof' because the deck is kept warm by the protective insulation, and this is the most efficient construction, recommended for new installations. A 'cold roof' is so-called when the insulation is above the ceiling and sandwiched within the structure, and this requires good ventilation to make sure no moisture is trapped inside. At least a 50mm (2in) gap between the top of the insulation and the deck, ventilated from both ends, is required. For warm-roof construction, there's a vapour control layer (VCL) fixed beneath the insulation, and this prevents movement of potentially damaging moisture into the structure. The top surface of the waterproofing material is usually covered with a mineral surfaced layer inherent in the felt, as a 'capsheet', alternatively a layer of mineral chippings may be bedded into an adhesive/bitumen type material to bond it to the top, both to give protection from ultraviolet light degradation and also from fire from external sources.

Metals and Asphalt for Covering Flat Roofs

Metals were used in the past, and are still used in some applications today (see Chapter 5) for details).

Roof joists supported by joist hangers set into the wall, with firring on top.

Roofing Felts

The different kinds are described in Chapter 9.

CHIMNEYS/CHIMNEY-BREASTS/GUTTERS

In an older house, the chimney-breast was a rectangular block built on the inside (occasionally on the outside) of an outside wall, from the ground floor up through the first floor, narrowing to a chimney within the roof space area and emerging at the top of the house. The fireplaces are fitted against and within holes in these breasts in rooms. Frequently, in Victorian and earlier houses, one ground-floor fireplace accommodated the kitchen range, and in medieval houses an inglenook fireplace was of considerable size, incorporating seats.

Often you'll see a chimney-breast that has been removed, and this is usually evident as a box-shape at ceiling height, which is cut off at a 45-degree angle, rather than being sliced off at right angles. If parts of a chimney-breast are removed, attention has to focus on what is above, because if a lower chimney-breast is removed incorrectly, the entire weight of the chimney-breast and chimney above is unsupported and could possibly collapse.

A fine spiral staircase. Julian Owen Associates Architects

Gutters

These were originally made of lead, then of cast iron, and now are mostly made of plastic, although cast-iron guttering is still being made. Essentially, they are lengths of material of semicircular cross-section, fixed at the eaves below the roof, screwed via brackets onto the fascia board. Fixed to form a gentle slope, at their lowest point is a hole that plugs into a 'downpipe', leading down to a soakaway or the main drains. Sometimes more than one downpipe leads to a hopper (collection box) that itself is fitted to a downpipe. It can be problematic repairing old guttering if the modern equivalent is of a different size – sometimes you have to renew all of it. New cast-iron guttering is extremely expensive but can look very attractive on a suitable building, and is sometimes required for a listed building, since guttering may have to be replaced 'like-for-like'. Old and corroded cast-iron guttering can be very hazardous, because if fixings have failed it can fall and could certainly cause injury.

STAIRS AND STAIRCASES

Prior to the end of the 1500s, stairs were considered more as an add-on, but after that time they were regarded as a feature, with magnificent framed, oak staircases with carved newel posts. The majority are made of wood, but there are also stone stairs in large Victorian houses, and banisters can be of iron.

WINDOWS

Evolving from glass-less wind eyes, or 'lights', under the eaves and covered with parchment or waxed paper, in the late-1500s valuable leaded-light glass was used in non-opening iron-framed windows, then later in side-opening wooden casement windows. In the late 1600s vertically sliding 'sash' windows arrived and were popular for two centuries, and are still used and produced today. Initially, glass could only be made in small-sized pieces, joined by lead strips (leaded lights), and later windows were made incorporating glazing bars of metal or wood, that divided the glazed area; after 1865, large panels of glass could be produced, ending the necessity for dividing window panes. If you have old, inefficient,

---

Types of Staircase

Cantilevered: where stairs are fixed to a wall on one side but are unsupported at the other, e.g. with internal stone stairs, where the end is firmly fixed into the wall.

Closed string: where the string hides the treads.

Dogleg: a flight that has a 180-degree turn at a half landing.

Geometric: normally a cantilevered staircase, its side string winding up around an open well, without newel posts.

Mast newel staircase: spiral staircase with a centre newel that rises up through the building.

Open well: where two flights that turn as a dogleg are separated to give a spacious effect. The straight connecting section is called a quarter landing.

Open/cut string: where sides of treads are visible at the side, above the string.

Window fitters having removed a rotten bay window, with a steel support temporarily supporting the bays above.

Types of Window

Bay: with sizeable side-panels so as to form a projection outwards from a room, thereby adding extra space and increasing the light.

Bow: window that projects outwards in a shallow curve.

Casement: side-opening windows (usually opening on one or sometimes on both sides), with iron or timber frames.

Crittall window: casement-style steel windows first made in the 1930s by the company Crittalls, now being manufactured in the original way. These are simply flat-glass panels mounted into panes surrounded by framing with a T cross-section to accommodate glazing either side.

Dormer: window in a roof, built out as a structure with its own mini roof.

Fixed light: medieval construction, whereby leaded lights are either framed by wrought-iron rectangles or fixed directly to the outside. Non-opening.

Sash: two wooden (or originally metal) frames surrounding glass panels, which slide against each other vertically. The single-sliding sash is where the upper light is fixed and only the lower can slide, whereas the more usual double-sliding sash is where both frames move in tandem with each other, counter-balanced by a system of ropes or chains on pulleys and weights; these are housed at the sides, within the frame. They are locked closed where they meet at the centre by means of a catch.

UPVC: modern 'plastic' windows.

---

sash windows there are a number of companies who can repair them for you so they meet modern insulation standards, or you can buy new matching styles of sash window. Not all plastic (UPVC) windows are of good quality but those that are will not rot, and, due to integral metal structures where support is needed, are perfectly adequate structurally. Bear in mind, if you're replacing windows, that they need to have a FENSA certificate, or alternatively the local authority Building Control Department have to certify that they meet the current building regulations.

Window fitters at work.

CHAPTER 5

Subsidence, Wall and Flat-Roof Problems

SUBSIDENCE

This means a building's movement downwards, caused by a reduction in the previously existing support beneath its foundations. Crucially it's a relatively rare problem, although buildings on clay ground with conventional 'footing' foundations are more susceptible to subsidence during very dry summers than those on sandy, gravelly or silty soils. In the majority of cases subsidence can be cured without major building supportive works, termed underpinning. Frequent causes are changes in the soil's water content, nearby trees or shrubs, or leaking drains adding moisture underground or washing away of the ground beneath the foundations; attention to these factors cures the situation in the long term.

Cracks are perfectly usual in buildings – indeed virtually all structures have them and they are perfectly normal; you should only be concerned if they are particularly noticeable, and getting larger. All soil, clay in particular, contains a variable amount of moisture, dependent on rainfall, and within usual limits supports the weight of the building above it perfectly adequately – in clay, when there's less or more moisture than usual, problems may occur; sandy soils, on the other hand, can have material washed away, creating voids.

Avoid unscrupulous 'professional' subsidence specialist building companies that tout for business, warning you in a hot summer to examine your house for cracks. This is nonsensical advice because a subsidence problem is never something you have to search for, it is usually glaringly obvious, and any company soliciting work and trying to scare you is likely to have a vested interest in finding problems that are not there. Generally speaking, if you are worried about any building problem whatsoever, especially something as potentially serious as subsidence, it's best to go to a completely independent structural engineer or building surveyor and pay for their assessment. If you seriously suspect that you may have a subsidence problem, the correct course of action is to inform your insurance company – however, don't do this without careful thought, as any query of this nature, even if afterwards found to completely groundless, will be recorded, and may put a question mark against the building on the insurer's file.

Insurance is the major consideration. Most policies cover subsidence damage (albeit often with an excess figure), but making a claim can have

A subsidence nightmare scenario. Target Fixings Ltd

Large crack in this brickwork, with a measuring device fixed across, so as to monitor it over time. Coopers Engineering Consultants

unpleasant ramifications, since the policy may not cover a further claim, and without this type of insurance, any future sale could be blighted. However, there are ways you can protect yourself (*see below*) and you do have rights. Most experts advise that if you suspect subsidence you should immediately tell your insurance company, and the companies may stipulate that they should be informed at an early stage. However, unless you are an expert, you cannot know for sure, so if there are doubts, an independent survey could be an advisable first step, even though you will have to pay for it.

ABOVE: **Major crack splitting bricks apart, near a corner.** Coopers Engineering Consultants

LEFT: **A diagonal crack, running along mortar lines.** Coopers Engineering Consultants

Closer view of wall with diagonal crack.
Coopers Engineering Consultants

Closer view of cracks near the bottom of a wall. Coopers Engineering Consultants

Cracks near the bottom of a wall.
Coopers Engineering Consultants

Cracks alongside a projecting concrete support in a wall. Coopers Engineering Consultants

BOTTOM LEFT: **Crack on wall continues underneath the roof area.**

TOP: **Cracks beneath a projecting concrete support.** Coopers Engineering Consultants

BOTTOM: **Another view of cracks beside a projecting concrete support.**
Coopers Engineering Consultants

Subsidence Facts

All Houses Have Cracks
Most often they are of no significance; rendering mortar itself, in particular, is prone to cracking, and in most cases the wall behind is unaffected – render cracks should be repaired, however, as they can allow in moisture that then cannot easily escape.

If Subsidence is Diagnosed by an Expert
For the vast majority of cases this can be cured by repairing broken drains or removing nearby trees or shrubbery.

Expert Quote 1

An experienced surveyor advises:

> Walls expand and contract because of thermal variations, giving cracks that are perfectly natural and do not matter, while some cracks could signify past subsidence that has ended. Most people are concerned if a crack becomes more than 5mm wide, so if you have such a problem, especially if it's a tapered crack that's getting worse, then you should definitely inform your insurance company. Cracks of over 25mm may be serious, however a lot of subsidence is not serious – it's natural movement shrinkage, thermal movement and, in many cases, movement does not matter. Ideally, filling of cracks can be with epoxy-based mortars or fillers (if suitable) to help restore the wall's strength, rather than using standard fillers.

RIGHT: **Thermal or shrinkage crack – because it has constant width over its length.**
Brian Clancy

ABOVE: **This small crack in brickwork is too small to be of any significance.**

RIGHT: **Large diagonal crack in a brick wall.**
KMASS Consulting Engineers: www.kmass.co.uk

Expert Quote 2

Graham Abrey, surveyor of Ingram Consultancy (*see* Contacts):

All buildings and structures continually move to varying degrees by expansion and contraction of the building materials and movements of the subsoil below foundations cause by seasonal changes, but these movements are typically very small and may not be readily visible. The domestic buildings of the Edwardian and earlier periods are likely to be flexible structures, provided they are built incorporating lime mortar, and more readily accommodate minor building movements than those made using cement mortars. Typical defects seen following subsidence are cracking of the mortar joints, displacement of window, door heads and arches and cracking of plaster finishes. To a lesser extent there could be fracturing of brickwork, stone and terracotta. Matching materials should always be used for repair. Resins can be used where additional strength is required for a repair. These are available in varying consistencies, so as to provide a way of controlling their degree of absorption into a fracture. Hydraulic lime grouts can be too liquid, running through the cracks and spreading to unintended locations, or else too thick or gritty, impeding their penetrability. Always find a craftsman who is familiar with the use of whatever materials your engineer or surveyor specifies.

If Your House Needs Underpinning

In this unlikely event it is usual for the insurance company to cover the costs of the remedial works and, if considered reasonably necessary, alternative rental living arrangements, storage of furniture and the costs for redecoration afterwards of the superstructure areas affected by the subsidence.

The Insurance Excess

With most insurance policies there is an excess (usually around £1,000 as of 2011).

After Work Has Been Completed

When remedial work has been completed it is vital to get a Certificate of Structural Adequacy, and you should get an undertaking from the insurance company to 'maintain insurance on the property for the foreseeable future' at normal market rates and that they will allow that to continue for the benefit of a prospective future purchaser who satisfactorily completes a standard proposal form. Without these documents a future sale could be blighted.

If the Claim is Repudiated
by the Insurance Company

Get a letter from your insurer explaining why subsidence is not a factor and what are the considered alternative causes for the symptoms. If you are not satisfied with the explanation of your insurer, then consider getting an independent 'second opinion' from an experienced structural or civil engineer or building surveyor.

Legal Obligations

The law is that if you know you have a subsidence problem – or any other major structural defect – and you deliberately cover up the evidence to sell a house, you have committed an offence under the Trades Descriptions Act. However, repairing a crack that you have no reason to suppose is caused by subsidence (or any other major defect) is obviously perfectly legal.

Role of the Insurance Company

If you notify the insurance company, then this suspicion is recorded, even if proved groundless, and could affect future insurance premiums and sales. However, if you note any evidence internally or externally to suggest your property may have subsidence, it is a condition of most insurance policies that prompt notification is required. The key is to think carefully before you do anything.

The Older the Better

Older properties, over 150 years old, rarely show signs of significant movement because they have been there long enough to have encountered most types of soil conditions. On the other hand, Victorian and pre-Victorian houses are likely to have relatively shallow foundations, meaning they are more susceptible to soil changes; since about 1950 building regulations have ensured much deeper foundations are mandatory – and, since the 1980s that new domestic property takes into account the presence of any existing trees on or near the site.

It's Unlikely to be as Bad as It May Look

About 80 per cent of damage caused by subsidence turns out to be no more than cosmetic, but this can be significantly higher in years of 'drought', meaning one of prolonged hot summers and/or dry winters.

External Underpinning

There are many situations where underpinning can be done externally, and internal finishes don't need to be disturbed.

Internal Underpinning

When internal work is needed the homeowner may have to vacate the premises for anything up to between six weeks and six months. Internal works can cause damage to internal decorations and exacerbates cracks, requiring substantial redecoration afterwards.

Symptoms of Subsidence

Cracks

These are usually diagonal and tapering, with the widest edge at the top. This widest edge is often at the corner of a house or top of a wall, or edge of a door or window. These cracks may travel around openings. External cracks are mirrored internally: even cavity walls are affected on both skins – though the cracks inside may not coincide exactly with those outside.

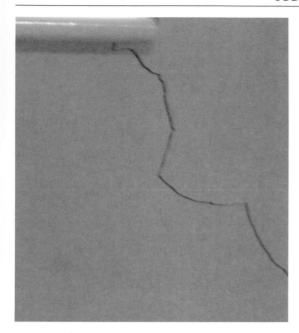

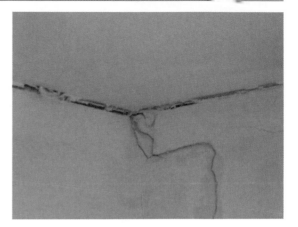

Cracks in an internal wall, continuing along the ceiling. KMASS Consulting Engineers: www.kmass.co.uk

ABOVE: **Crack in an internal wall.**
KMASS Consulting Engineers: www.kmass.co.uk

BELOW: **Large crack in an internal wall.**
KMASS Consulting Engineers: www.kmass.co.uk

Other Possible Signs of Subsidence
- Dips in the horizontal coursing of brick or stone with attendant cracking.
- Sloping floors (use a spirit-level to check); however, suspended floors do sag naturally, so don't be misled by this.
- Sloping lintels (concealed supports above windows and doors), also distorted doors.
- Bulges in solid walls, though this can also be caused by the wrong type of repointing.
- Doors or windows sticking for no apparent reason.
- Rippling wallpaper, not caused by damp.
- Cracks caused by 'heave' (the reverse of subsidence) are sometimes wider at the bottom than at the top.

Causes of Ground Movement

Leaking Drains
Clay soil can swell or slump as a result of the extra water, and sandy soils might have fine particles washed away, leaving holes. Additionally, movement because of subsidence can of course break drains, meaning the primary cause of subsidence is less easy to diagnose. The use of plastic underground drainage pipes is relatively recent, and if your drains are more than around thirty years old they will be made of glazed stoneware – these are in the form of lengths of piping, joined at regular intervals

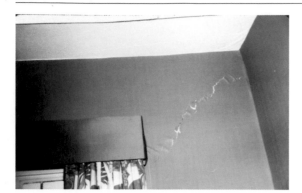

Typical subsidence crack – internal. Brian Clancy

(about every 1m/3ft), using lime or cement to effect the seal. These pipes and their joints are very hard and brittle, and any ground movement can cause the drain or joint to crack, also they can deteriorate and break down. Have a CCTV drain test to ascertain their condition. Tree roots can also grow into old drain pipes, blocking and breaking them. Another possible cause can be discharge of rainwater that doesn't disperse where it's supposed to, especially if this is concentrated over one area of soil near the house.

Trees

Some tree roots absorb water from deep levels of clay and, coupled with periods of dry weather, can result in soil changes; conversely, if a tree is removed heave can occur, due to the extra water. In a recent survey about 70 per cent of subsidence claims on shrinkable clay soils were attributed to trees and shrubs near the property taking away water. Broad-leaved or deciduous trees need more water than evergreen (coniferous) ones. An oak or willow tree can have roots spreading up to 30–40m (100–130ft), and ideally neither should be close to a property.

Filled Ground

If your house was built on a landfill site there's the possibility of collapse, decomposition or slump of organic material in the soil; alternatively, some non-inert substances can change chemically, to cause heave.

Mining Excavations

If your house is built in a mining area, then remember that ancient mine workings can collapse because of factors such as decay of wooden pit-props that supported the structures or just consolidation of the ground disturbed by the mining activity.

Typical excavation for mass concrete block underpinning. Brian Clancy

Underpinning – reinforced concrete beam on piles – ready for shuttering and casting.
Brian Clancy

Nearby Excavations
Excavations made near a building can cause direct ground movement as the ground beneath your property collapses into the adjacent excavations if they are not properly supported, or can affect the local water table that may be under your property.

Changes in the Water Table
Drainage schemes can alter this.

Swallow Holes, Sinks or Gulls
These are cavities formed in the subsoil by percolating water, principally in chalky soil.

TOP: **Large willow tree close to property – very suspect, if clay substratum.** Brian Clancy

BELOW: **Trees near properties – possible subsidence problems, if on clay substrata.** Brian Clancy

Very shallow foundations to property. Brian Clancy

Chemical Attack
Chemicals in the ground can either attack foundation brickwork (subsidence) or cause heave in the soil.

Underpinning

Not so simple as it sounds because adding completely inflexible foundations to a relatively 'flexible' older property could cause additional problems. Partial underpinning can also do harm if not judged carefully. For these reasons you obviously need an experienced structural engineer to plan the most suitable remedial works.

Types of Underpinning

Mass Concrete Underpinning/
Traditional Underpinning
Digging by hand below the existing foundations and putting concrete into the cavity, to add depth to the original foundations. Holes are dug and filled in separate blocks or bays, thereby leaving areas of original ground for support throughout the operation.

Beam and Pier
Where an area of masonry is removed from a

Concrete block underpinning excavations. Brian Clancy

ABOVE: **Bar flex wraps around the helical pile, this is a method of pile and beam repair.**
Target Fixings Ltd

RIGHT: **The Heli Pile rig is a small machine.**
Target Fixings Ltd

wall's base, then a concrete beam is cast into this void. This horizontal concrete beam below the wall is either cast above, or in place of, the existing footings. An area of masonry is removed from the base of the wall, which is temporarily propped, then the concrete beam is cast into this void. Large areas beneath the beam are excavated vertically at intervals in order to cast large supportive piers at strategic intervals along the length of the new beams.

Piles
Circular holes drilled into the soil and filled with fine aggregate concrete. Either existing foundations are broken through to drill these or else holes in soil are drilled from concrete supports set at right angles to the base of the wall. There are also newer mini-piling systems. Sometimes steel or plastic cases are first inserted, to act as a sleeve for the mix.

Beam and Pile
Similar to beam and pier, but the beams are cast with extensions built out at right angles so they can be drilled and filled with concrete either side

of the wall, so areas directly beneath the footings don't need to be excavated. These piles and beams are inserted either side of footings, and there is no need to disturb the soil beneath the foundations.

Pressure Grouting
Liquid mortar is injected at pressure straight into the ground, filling any voids between hardcore, rocks or granular materials. Ineffective in clay soils. Pressure grouting needs to be carefully controlled or drains and other services may be blocked by the grout.

Insurance
Many insurance companies used to refuse to offer subsidence cover if a property had a history of subsidence, possibly blighting a future sale if you had underpinning work done, although there are ways you can protect yourself (*see above*). The Subsidence Claims Advisory Bureau (SCAB) can help you find an insurer, for instance if you want to buy somewhere with such a possible subsidence

Expert Quote 1

Jon Cawley, Property Claims Director at Zurich Insurance (*see* Contacts):

> Properties over 150 years old rarely show signs of recent significant movement, as they have encountered most types of soil condition over the years. It's rare for subsidence cracks to compromise the safety of a building. The majority of damage caused by subsidence turns out to be no more than cosmetic, though it can look alarming.

Expert quote 2

Robert C. Hooker of SCAB (*see* Contacts):

> The majority of insurance companies will decline new business to cover for subsidence damage if a property has a past history of subsidence or where a claim has been made on a previous company's policy. The existing insurers may even increase the premium as they perceive that there is an increased risk of exposure, even if they have paid to have the house underpinned. There are specialists who can help – Subsidence Claims Advisory Bureau Ltd with their associated broker can find alternatives from a panel of underwriters to find the best deal for you. Their Previously Underpinned Properties Scheme (PUPS) relies upon them making a visual inspection of the property to assess the current condition where there has been past subsidence. They will assess if the work is all right, or might recommend remedial action or precautions that can be taken.
>
> Keeping a record of what, when and why repairs have been undertaken is also essential following a subsidence damage claim and you should ensure that the supervising engineer or loss adjuster issues a Certificate of Structural Adequacy; this form was devised by the Institute of Structural Engineers and it will establish the dates when events took place.

problem. When remedial work has been completed it is vital to get a Certificate of Structural Adequacy, and you should also get an undertaking to 'maintain insurance on the property for the foreseeable future' at normal market rates that will be allowed to continue for the benefit of a prospective future purchaser. Without these documents you could blight a future sale or, in case of repudiation, you need a letter documenting the reasons. If a claim is repudiated by the insurance company, insist on getting a letter explaining why subsidence is not a factor and what is the considered cause for the symptoms in the opinion of your insurer. If you disagree with the repudiation, get a second opinion from an independent engineer or surveyor who is experienced in the field.

Loss Adjusters

- Employed by insurance companies, a loss adjuster's role is to gather facts, diagnose situations, suggest solutions and liaise with homeowners.
- Their brief is to reduce the insurance company's commitment, while also being fair to the homeowner.
- They are sometimes also qualified structural or civil engineers. An engineer employed by the insurance company assesses the problem separately in order to diagnose causes and suggest cures.
- Due to mergers, etc., there are now only a handful of engineering contracting companies that specialize in subsidence reparation work.
- In an attempt to reduce their insurance company's liability, a loss adjuster may recommend lengthy 'monitoring' of cracks before advocating action, or even repudiating valid claims. In such instances, when you disagree with the loss adjuster's decision, you have the right to have your own independent survey done (but this is at your own expense). Monitoring periods should usually be for about twelve months (or less) and rarely if ever for more than twenty-four months.

Expert Quote

Brian Clancy, Past President of the Institution of Structural Engineers and Chairman of their Subsidence Task Group:

Your insurance company has the expertise to diagnose causes properly. It is best to approach them in the first instance, rather than a structural engineer or surveyor, as you'll avoid the danger of calling in people who have a vested interest in finding problems. But if you are genuinely not satisfied with your insurer's decision, then you may wish to have a second opinion, for which you might have to pay.

It is occasionally necessary to monitor cracks as a check before remedial work has been done, for up to a period of six months to a year The Institution of Structural Engineers recommendations are that no monitoring should exceed a year, except in exceptional cases (perhaps 1 in 100), when it could be two years, but never longer. A trained person can normally diagnose the cause of subsidence by looking at the direction, the geometry, the pattern, etc., of cracks, leading to a focal cause, such as a tree, bush or leaking drain.

Subsidence has existed for thousands of years. Many of the big cathedrals either fell down because of subsidence or fire. In 1972/73 insurance companies actually started to give subsidence cover as part of their normal policy cover. Prior to that, if you had subsidence it was just a normal maintenance matter, which you attended to with your builder or structural engineer. The problem was that from 1972 the cover was given away for nothing. Then in 1975/76 there were two relatively hot summers and a relatively dry winter in between, so buildings were cracking and insurance companies, in fairness to them,

dealt with the matter very generously. Although they weren't expecting so many claims, they were fair. When the surge came in 1975/76 they found they were making a colossal loss on subsidence claims. They immediately turned round and said that in future they weren't giving cover for properties that had previously suffered from subsidence.

Generally speaking, 80 per cent of subsidence claims occur in the south-east of England area for two reasons. One – because there are more people and properties in that area. Two – it's where you do get the bands of shrinkable clay. In 95 per cent of cases the cause of subsidence is trees and bushes desiccating the ground, i.e. shrinkable clay, or, in areas where there may or may not be clay, leaking drains. On the whole, clay problems tend to cause 60–70 per cent of cases, and drain problems account for 30 per cent. And in dry summers, the clay problems increase significantly, probably by up to 85–90 per cent, whereas drain problems are proportionately less frequent, more like 10–20 per cent.

The aim is always to avoid underpinning whenever possible. An insurance company's approach is that they normally ask three questions. One: there's a crack. Is it continuing? If not, then treat it cosmetically and that's the end of it. If it's continuing then, two: 'Can we identify the cause and rectify and/or remove it?' If yes, then we get on with it. Questions three is: 'Have we got any other option than to underpin?' If not, then we underpin.

Remedial work done by members of the Association of Specialist Underpinning Contractors (ASUCplus) is covered by a twelve-year indemnity defects insurance guarantee that is independent of your own household insurance. Even if the company that did the work goes bust, the guarantee is covered by ASUCplus, and this can be passed on to any future buyer; but remember that warranties and guarantees are only as good as the organization issuing them.

For previously underpinned properties, the Subsidence Claims Advisory Bureau (SCAB) (see

Contacts) offer to do a survey of the property, and if the underpinning work is deemed adequate by them, will act as brokers to get you a fair insurance deal. They either guarantee that the work is all right, or might recommend remedial action to bring it up to the correct standard.

Trade Body

The Association of Specialist Underpinning Contractors (ASUCplus) (www.asuc.org.uk; 01420 471613) represents leading specialist underpinning contractors.

CAVITY WALL-TIE FAILURE

Most houses built during the last century, from about 1920, have cavity walls, meaning that two walls are built beside each other with a cavity of approximately 50mm (2in) between them. Wall ties are basically lengths of metal, wire or strips of twisted metal (and occasionally other materials) that link the two walls together, so as to make a combined structure that's rigid and reasonably weatherproof and provides a better degree of thermal insulation than an equivalent solid wall: the outer leaf of the wall gets wet, not the inner. Wall ties are incorporated into the horizontal brick mortar courses of both walls at regular intervals – about 900mm (3ft) horizontally and 450mm (18in) vertically. Wall-tie failure is a condition when the tie materials break down, normally as a result of corrosion, thereby allowing the two leafs of the wall to separate, possibly with catastrophic results. Unsupported outer walls are susceptible to high winds, and, in a worst case scenario, could collapse.

Black ash mortar, used in some localities, is known to have a deleterious effect on cavity wall-ties.

You are likely to have a cavity wall if your brickwork is built in 'stretcher bond', that is the long brick sides visible, indicating the 'half-brick thickness' of the outer skin. However, if there are alternate, short bricks (meaning they're been laid end-on with the header visible), it is likely to be a solid wall, but do not be fooled: sometimes this solid brick 'effect' was done for appearances' sake. If your wall is rendered, drill a hole over 130 mm (5in) deep and you'll feel the drill 'drop' through into the cavity beyond here. A cavity wall will typically be 265mm (10½in) to 280mm (11in) thick, while a solid wall is likely to be between 230mm (9in) and 340mm (13½in) thick. However, plastering on solid walls may increase their thickness to close to that of a cavity wall, so the drill test is the most reliable. For domestic buildings built after 1930, cavity walls were the norm for external main walls.

Symptoms of Cavity Wall-Tie Failure

- Horizontal cracking of the mortar joints or rendering in particular areas, possibly opening up to 3–4mm or more approximately every fifth or sixth course.
- Bulging of masonry – sometimes noticeable at heads of window and door openings, where new gaps and voids show between frames and brickwork to cavity.

The inside of a cavity wall, showing the ties.
Property Care Association

Expert Quote

John Dee, of Peter Cox (*see* Contacts):

It's more work if you have to physically remove all the old ties, rather than protecting them with foam. When the wall is of hard engineering bricks with narrow mortar courses, there is often no alternative but to break out and replace bricks individually. Cavity walls first started coming into being, typically in the 1870s. They tended to be in the more exposed conditions, coastal, west coast and south of England, and the east coast. They offered greater protection from the rain, and great thermal protection. From then onwards their use started gaining momentum, but it was not until 1920s and 1930s that cavity walls became more generally used. The main type used between 1870 and 1930 was the iron fishtail type. There's a problem with black-ash mortar having a particularly deleterious effect on the metal – you tend to find this used in mining areas – though I would say that this black-ash mortar effect tends to be exaggerated. The material doesn't always corrode the ties, it depends on the tie and what sort of protection has been given to it. Always employ a reputable company for inspection, diagnosis and remedial work.

   To deal with the redundant and possibly corrosively expanding ties, we'd cut a gap all the way around the part of the tie in the outer leaf, so that the tie is basically doing nothing, just hangs there loose in the outer leaf (the inner leaf doesn't usually cause a problem). Then we'd normally fill the created void around the tie with structural foam, polyurethane foam, which fills the gap and protects the tie from moisture, stops further rusting and also stops the tie continuing to expand, or if there is any expansion, this is cushioned by the foam. Some have to be completely removed, which involves a lot of work. Prior to 1945 there were no regulations regarding protection of ties. You find all sorts of weird things in cavity walls – we treated a property up here and all the ties were made from corroded half horseshoes!'

- Brown/red iron oxide rust stains as spots on the façade or damp patches on internal walls.
- 'White rust' marks where zinc-galvanized round steel oxidizes.

Old Wall-Ties – What They Are

Ties
Early types (1870–1930) were usually made of wrought iron, later on of steel. Some were protected by bitumen, while others were zinc galvanized. For the past thirty years stainless steel ties have normally been used and now nylon ones are gaining popularity, but prior to 1980 wall ties were either 'fishtail' or 'vertical twist' ties: flat-section iron with a twist in the centre (to allow water to drip within the cavity) and splayed tails at each end, intended to bed neatly into a mortar joint. When fishtail iron ties corrode the metal expands because of this (up to seven times its size), and cracking of the surrounding mortar can result. Another popular type of wall tie is called a butterfly or double triangle tie, made of galvanized wire twisted in such a way as to form a butterfly shape, with a twisted-together joint that hangs downwards into the cavity; the idea of this is that if water tries to cross the cavity from outside leaf of the wall to the inner leaf then it'll be channelled along this stub of wire and drop off. Butterfly ties can simply snap off within the cavity, leaving bulging walls while not causing cracking. Older houses even (rarely) had ties made of slate or tile.

   These ties are there to provide support from the inner, load-bearing wall to the outer façade, the two leaves joined by ties act in combination to resist the effects of wind suction and compression. They must be made so as to prevent water transfer across the cavity and to be flexible enough to allow all differential movement between the two walls without stressing the mortar connection.

Rules for Replacement
- Apart from making initial limited exploratory excavation, generally new replacement ties should be installed before the corroded ones are removed and/or masonry is disfigured.
- Don't use expandable mechanical fixings when working with soft and friable masonry materials.

- Some cavity-fill insulation materials may interact badly with some wall-tie systems.

Process of Replacement – If Problems of Tie Corrosion or Failure are Suspected

Diagnosis
- Locate typical existing metal ties using a metal detector.
- Insert a fibre-optic endoscope into the wall cavity to assess the ties' condition at their central parts.
- Ideally, to assess a tie's overall condition, the brick above the tie should be removed to see the embedded end's corrosion.
- Sample ties are removed from the wall and examined for their degree of corrosion.

Insertion of Stainless Steel Ties
Ties are firmly fixed inside pre-drilled holes in the inner and outer leaves. This is either by mechanical means, where an expandable collar is tightened from the outside to effect a compression grip, alternatively thixotropic resin adhesive is pumped into the holes, into which the steel is set. Sometimes a combination of these methods is used.

Process
1. Holes drilled to a gauged depth from the outer wall across the cavity and into the inner leaf of the wall.
2. Holes are cleared of debris and dust.
3. The replacement wall tie, made of strong stainless steel or robust plastic, is inserted from the outside and bonded into both the inner leaf wall hole and then in the outer leaf.
4. Ties are tested for security before finally making good.
5. Old ties are removed completely or encased in injected styrene so as to allow a cushion for expansion.
6. However, when the wall is made of hard engineering bricks with narrow mortar courses there is often no alternative but to break out and replace bricks individually.

Finishing-Off
1. External holes in brickwork, render or mortar joints need to be made good with mortar or mastic (of a matching colour) or original brick drilling powder can be replaced, using resin adhesive. Complete external repointing may be a better option so as to avoid an unsightly 'patchwork' effect.
2. Attention to any internal timber that has been disturbed.
3. Rebuilding of any brickwork necessary.
4. Reinstatement of disturbed insulation.

Expert Quote

Steve Hodgson, General Manager of the Property Care Association (PCA):

The PCA is the trade association that provides accreditation and support to specialists in damp control, timber infestation, flood recovery, basement waterproofing, structural repair and condensation. Noted for its training and technical expertise, the PCA, incorporating the BWPDA, has been in existence for 75 years and ensures the highest standards are maintained by its members. When choosing a member of the PCA you can be certain that they have undergone rigorous ongoing checks to achieve and retain membership, an expert assessor with a wealth of experience and technical knowledge has audited every member and checked the quality of work on site. Regular technical, operational and procedural checks allow the PCA to give consumers the assurance that all members can deliver high quality service and peace of mind that can be supported by independently insured guarantees. Our rigorous application process ensures we allow only the industry's elite to join the association. Members are required to have or gain comprehensive industry recognized qualifications, are able to offer insurance backed guarantees, required to adhere to a formal code of conduct, a strict code of ethics, to adhere to minimum performance standards and are all licensed under the government's TrustMark scheme.

Professional Trade Bodies

It's very important that anyone you employ belongs to one of the below trade bodies:

The Wall-Tie Installers Federation (www.wtif. org.uk; 0151 494 2503) was formed in 1989 because there had been unscrupulous and/or incompetent companies who undertook this kind of work. Work done by their members is guaranteed and covers the entire installation – including the treatment of the existing installation and remedial works.

Property Care Association (PCA) (www.property-care.org; 0844 375 4301). Formerly part of the BWPDA, the PCA is described as the premier trade body for the structural waterproofing, wood preservation, damp-proofing, flood remediation and structural maintenance industries in the UK. On a personal note, I found the PCA to be an extremely helpful, agreeable and informative organization.

FLAT-ROOF PROBLEMS

What to Look For

Puddles Forming In and During Rain. This indicates sagging of the roofing material or its supporting structure, and is likely to lead to leaks. If the areas where puddles are forming occur along the lines of the roof joists, this could mean serious problems.

Blisters. Suggest that water may have entered the fabric of the roof waterproofing and is potentially serious, especially if these are getting bigger.

Roofing Felt Split Along the Line of the Boards Making Up the Roof Decking. This could mean that the timber decking substrata is moving because of internal decay caused by trapped moisture.

Felt Split Around Perimeter of Roof. Meaning there's movement between the walls and roof.

Layers of roofing felt, split at a corner, with lead flashing displaced above it.

Splits along roofing felt, likely to cause decay of the entire roof.

Splits and degeneration of old roofing felt.

Punctures to Felt. Caused typically by cable-clip installation: this is likely to lead to moisture ingress and inevitable rot.

Professional Trade Bodies

The National Federation of Roofing Contractors (NFRC) (www.nfrc.co.uk; 020 7638 7663) is the UK's largest roofing trade association representing over 70 per cent of the roofing industry by value, and offers a 'Find a contractor' service in your area for every kind of roofing work. By using an NFRC registered contractor you have the comfort of guaranteed protection and quality. NFRC actively ensures that members offer high standards of workmanship and sound business practice through a strict code of practice and independent vetting procedure including site inspections and adhering to the government-endorsed TrustMark standards. All NFRC trade members hold comprehensive insurance cover and insurance backed warranties are available.

The Flat Roofing Alliance (FRA) is a non-profit trade association and is a focus division of the NFRC, and exists to represent the interests of the reinforced bitumen membrane industry in terms of upholding product performance and installation standards so as to maximize quality, longevity and client satisfaction. The FRA produce and excellent book: *The Householders Guide to Flat Roofing* – contact them if you want a copy and they will let you know the costs.

CHAPTER 6

Damp Problems and Flooding

DAMP

Prior to the widespread use of cement, before around 1850, walls were built using mortar made from lime mixed with sand, which is a relatively soft, water-absorbent material; in fact these brick-bonding layers were designed to act as a wick, absorbing moisture and then relinquishing it to the atmosphere, according to the weather. Buildings were designed for rain to soak into their thick, solid, brick or stonework and mortars, penetrating to some extent, before evaporating naturally afterwards. Similarly, if the brick or stone outer surface was covered with render – again a mixture of lime and sand – this was also designed to absorb water and surrender it later, in just the same way. This approach to waterproofing a building is often referred to as the 'overcoat' approach, using the analogy of wearing a porous overcoat in the rain, then allowing it to dry.

After the mid-nineteenth century, cement replaced lime as the 'binder' in mortar and render mixes. This cement-and-sand combination produced a rock-hard substance that repelled water. Thus was born the 'raincoat' approach to construction, whereby buildings were intended to be waterproof. The new approach was that water should be repelled from the structure and hardly penetrate it at all. This is the approach to building today, whereby the building 'envelope' is sealed against moisture (the brick outer surface has a 'fire-skin' that repels water to some extent), and brick walls that are concealed are covered with waterproof cement-based renders that repel rain, and also painted with waterproof masonry

Horrific mould, damp and decay.
Property Care Association

Expert Quote

Robert Demaus (*see* Contacts), independent surveyor and lecturer on building faults:

What many people perceive as a damp problem in an old house may simply be moisture affecting their unsuitable decorations, rather than it having any serious effect on the structure. In many old houses moisture should evaporate from the interior surface of a wall, as well as the exterior, but is prevented by the impermeable paints and plasters so often used. I've seen far too many instances where expensive remedial work has been at best unnecessary and at worst seriously damaging. Bear in mind that, although most damp problems are very local, visible areas of damp often show up some distance away from the fault, or combination of faults, that cause them. Any fungus will die out when the moisture source is removed, and rarely needs chemical treatment. A comprehensively trained and experienced, independent surveyor is always better equipped to consider the building in its entirety.

Condensation on a wall, caused by the lead pipe behind the plaster.

paints. Further to this, after the late-1800s cavity-wall construction became the norm, whereby the wall was built as two sections with a cavity in between, so that any water that did penetrate the outer skin would drop downwards and not penetrate to the inner one. In each of these twin walls was a water-resistant layer about 15cm (6in) above ground level, called a damp-proof course (DPC), the first types normally made of two layers of black slate, later DPCs being made of an impervious rubbery plastic material. The idea of this was to prevent water rising up from the damp soil and entering the wall by capillary (suction) action.

Both these radically different building techniques work perfectly well, albeit that the pre-1850 'overcoat' type buildings tend to have slightly damp interior walls sometimes, something you just have to live with. However, mixing up the two approaches by trying to repair a lime-mortared house with cement-based materials always spells disaster, because waterproof materials used in a water-absorbing building act to trap moisture within the structure, with catastrophic results.

The Facts about Dampness in Houses

Straightforward Condensation is Often Mistaken for Rising or Penetrating Damp. What's more, condensation is generally much cheaper and easier to deal with, so make sure your surveyor gets it right.

Older Houses Have a Naturally Higher Level of Damp Than More Recent Constructions. Make sure whoever does your survey is familiar with the age of the property he or she is looking it, and that they make allowances accordingly.

Prolonged Dampness Can do Serious Damage. Examples being timber rot and infestations, plus extensive plaster degeneration.

Electrical Power Sockets in a Damp Wall Can be Deadly. Dampness can cause short-circuits that can lead to fires, and there's always the danger of electrocution if you are in the vicinity of water and electricity. If you have any doubts, do not touch or get close to the wall and consult a qualified electrician to check electrical safety.

Dampness Engenders Mould Growth. Mould alone does no harm, and can easily be removed by biocide, but the cause of the dampness must be rectified urgently.

Old Flagstone Floors Laid On to the Earth Will Always be Wet. If you remove lino from such a floor and find dampness this is to be expected, and the surface should be left open to the air, and not covered up or painted with impermeable sealants.

It is Natural for the Interior Walls of Pre-1850 Houses to Occasionally be Wet. This is because, like the outside walls, they are designed to become wet and dry naturally. Accordingly they should never be painted with impermeable paints, and you must use lime-wash or distemper, that allows the passage of water.

Moisture Meters are Not Always Totally Reliable. They work by measuring the electrical conductivity in the wall, which in turn is affected by the levels of water-induced hygroscopic salts; the presence of these salts may equally also be indicative only of a past, cured, dampness, because they may be trapped in the plaster. Previous damp measures could have included fitting aluminium wallpaper beneath covering papers, which would obviously drastically distort a reading.

A Surveyor's Report May State the Presence of Damp, and Say 'Further Investigation Necessary by a Specialist Firm'. If a damp-proofing company recommends expensive repair work you feel may not be required, always have other estimates and/or go to an independent damp consultant. Damp investigators frequently work for specialist damp-proofing companies, the majority of whom act with professional integrity. However, bear in mind that there can be unscrupulous characters who will have a vested interest in recommending expensive and unnecessary treatments.

Make Sure the Work is Guaranteed. This is necessary for when you come to sell the property.

Timber-Panelled Rooms. These can be especially susceptible to rot through damp, and require careful attention to avoid this.

Expert Quote 1

Peter Bannister, Building Pathologist, Assistant Director (Northern) of Hutton + Rostron Environmental Investigation Ltd:

> An historic building is still in existence because its construction was fundamentally sound. Modern ways of living – chiefly greater insulation and a lack of ventilation – are responsible for many instances of damaging condensations, the cause of dampness in around 70 per cent of cases.

If Your Building is Listed You Will Need Listed Building Consent. This is required before doing any major repairs, such as removing and replacing plaster, and failure to obtain it is a criminal offence. Contact one of your local council's Conservation Officers and explain the position, and he or she will guide you through the process.

Inept Repairs That Cause Damp

Using Incompatible Mortars and Renders

A great many damp problems have been caused to old buildings by the basic misunderstanding that you can use cement-based mortars (for re-pointing) and renders on a building that was built using

---

Expert Quote 2

John Moore, of John Moore Specialist Resins (*see* Contacts):

> Remember, a house is exactly the same as a person in some ways: it needs to keep warm, so that it can dry out naturally. Make sure your walls are clean, and remove moss and dirt. Also, if you've got ivy growing on your walls it might look splendid when it flowers for a couple of weeks of the year, but it's going to shield the wall from the sun and you'll never get rid of the dampness that's trapped behind it.

lime mortar, as explained above. When re-pointing is done with hard cement-based mortar to a wall built with lime mortar, water is drawn in behind the hard cement mortar surface, to penetrate right inside the building, where it is trapped behind the virtually waterproof mortar, causing major problems within the wall. Similarly, if you repair an absorbent lime-based render with a cement-based one, the same thing happens: water is drawn behind the layer and is trapped against the wall. In most circumstances it's unwise to put a damp-proof course into a wall that was never designed to have one. There may, however, be certain instances where some experts consider that this is advisable.

Repairing Timber-Framed Building Brickwork and Panel Infilling Material with Waterproof Material

Impervious water-sealing materials must not be used for these repairs, otherwise any water that penetrates from other areas will be trapped, unable to evaporate out.

Treating Old Flagstone Floors with Waterproof Seal or Paint or Covering Them with Lino

These must be painted with breathable materials, otherwise water rising up from the soil will be trapped in the material and cause degradation.

Adding Roofing Felt Where There Was None Previously

Roofs in many older houses were known to be not entirely waterproof, but because they also let through a draught of air, any entering water could easily evaporate. When roof coverings became more effecting and waterproof, it was (and still is) common practice to install a layer of roofing felt (which is waterproof) beneath the tiles (or slates). Many people install roofing felt under an old tiled roof, thinking it will improve its weatherproofing abilities and as a way to stop wind entering the loft space. This is likely to result in water entering the loft space and not evaporating, thereby causing damp problems.

Blocking Air-Bricks and Bridging DPCs

When a concrete path or patio is built alongside a house it is vital that its surface must be at least 150mm (6in) below the wall's DPC. If not, ground water will simply move sideways and back and rise up and soak the wall. Also, air-bricks that are at a low level in the wall, designed to ventilate the area beneath the floorboards, must not be blocked, or else rot and decay are likely to develop in the floor, because of the lack of ventilation.

A modern bitumen-type damp-proof course. Roy Ilott & Associates Ltd

*Applying Impermeable Plaster or Waterproof
Paint to Interior Walls That Have No DPC*
Because a wall without a DPC will always absorb a certain amount of water, both inside and outside, it needs to evaporate from the inside as well as the exterior. Applying a water seal in this way will lock the moisture in the wall, causing degeneration and decay. Most modern emulsion paints are impermeable, so for such walls it is necessary to use limewash or distemper.

*Putting in a New Concrete Floor
to Replace an Old Original Floor*
Stone floors in old houses were quite often laid directly on to the earth, and water from the soil was allowed to rise up naturally through the material and evaporate. If such a floor is replaced with a modern concrete type, incorporating a damp-proof membrane (*see* Glossary), then the soil water that is trapped below the DPM may be forced to the sides of the room and up the walls. One way of avoiding this is to incorporate ventilation panels at skirting-board level.

*Unconventional Rising Damp
Cures That Don't Work*
There are some reputable companies that offer various different ways of combating rising damp. Historically ceramic tubes have been used, as well as various methods of using electric current to drive moisture back down from a wall into the soil. These tend to be designed predominantly for unconventional houses, where the standard treatments are not appropriate; for instance, medieval castles or historic homes. Before employing one of these methods, be aware that not all companies are bona fide, and an old established firm is the safest choice. Always be guided by an independent damp surveyor, preferably someone who is not connected with the company.

Blocking-Off Fireplaces Incorrectly
A chimney-breast that is sealed in the room needs to have a ventilation panel, in order to allow any

**Very bad damp and mould on a wall,
particularly dangerous because the moisture is
so close to electric sockets.** Roy Ilott & Associates Ltd

Expert Quote

Ken Warren, of Warren Woodworm and Waverley Building Construction:

You should always attend to the external faults, which will reduce the water pressure into the wall. However, capillary attraction takes place at any time of the year, and the height of this capillary attraction will depend on many factors. If you have very hard or waterproof rendering/plaster on the internal surfaces, capillary attraction could, and has been known to, rise up to fourteen feet above ground level, decaying first-floor joist ends, but if the walls are left exposed internally and externally, the capillary rise will only be a few inches. That's why only breathable finishes should be used, such as lime plaster with only lime washes as a decorative finish. Emulsion paints should not be used on lime plaster as it will defeat the object of enabling the walls to breathe.

moisture in the chimney to evaporate, otherwise dampness could occur in the wall.

Types of Damp in Buildings
The different kinds of damp are often confused, and it's important to distinguish which yours is.

Penetrating Damp
This is where rainwater actually penetrates through the wall into the interior, through a gap in the structure. Once the cause is found and corrected, no further repairs are needed unless decay or degradation of materials has resulted.

What to Look For
Localized wet patches on interior walls, especially noticeable after wet weather.

Causes
It occurs whenever a repeated heavy flow of water passes over one small area in a wall or roof. Causes can include broken lead flashings around a parapet wall or chimney, water sucked through the wall as a result of capillary action after a cracked render draws moisture in, or incorrect pointing has been done, or there is a crack or gap in the mortar itself. When re-pointing, mortars always have to match the original in terms of type of sand and binder and their constituent ratios, and there are companies that offer a mortar-matching service. Thick stone walls sometimes have a core of rubble, and this can become completely saturated, acting as a reservoir for water. A soakaway (*see* Glossary) can become blocked, causing water to 'back up' and overflow against the building. Leaking gutters and downpipes might direct water to one particular spot. A water, or central heating, pipe within the wall may be leaking – in this instance you'll notice localized dampness, discoloration, softness or crumbling of plaster, or even water droplets on the surface.

Cures
Repair broken building components, or re-do incorrect rendering and pointing.

Rising Damp

This is when water is sucked into the wall's structure from the ground, typically affecting only the lower part of the wall. Hygroscopic – meaning water-attractant – salts from the soil are also drawn up into the wall and through to the wall's internal plaster. These remain after the damp problem is cured, and they attract moisture in the room and can also ulcerate plaster. It is for this reason that it's necessary to replace this contaminated plaster with hard, waterproof plaster.

What to Look For
Rising salt-edged stain of dampness with clearly defined edges on the lower parts of the wall, tide-mark stains on wallpaper and/or feathery crystals of white salt deposits.

Causes
Post-1875 houses can have a compromised DPC, either because of breakdown or because it is bridged by soil levels building up higher than where

Rising damp on an internal wall, causing wallpaper to shrink and come off.
Property Care Association

Classic signs of rising damp on an internal wall, notice rotten skirting on bottom right.
Property Care Association

it is, or else preventing water's evaporation from the base of the wall. A concrete path around a house can cause 'splash up' during rainfall that can soak the wall above the DPC, preventing it draining away downwards. External render that completely covers over the DPC will allow water to travel through and bypass it. A problem with 1930s to 1960s houses can be when the wall cavity becomes filled above DPC level with mortar, dropped down from above during construction, therefore bridging the DPC. What is more, pre-1900 houses with suspended timber floors often were built straight on to the earth, with no concrete oversite to seal the soil, so water-soaked soil can virtually touch the bottom of timbers.

Cures

Remove soil to 150mm (6in) below the DPC level. You can ascertain where the DPC is by, if necessary, knocking off a section of paint or rendering

Expert Quote

Ken Warren, of Warren Woodworm and Waverly Building Construction:

Within the capillary damp, there will also be an element of hygroscopic salts, which are normally absorbed in the moisture from ground moisture or dislodged from the building materials from which the property is constructed. As the moisture from the capillary rise evaporates, the salts that are solid migrate to the surface of the plaster. As these salts are hygroscopic, they will continue to absorb moisture from the air. If you only insert a new damp-proof course this will only deal with 60 per cent of the problem, 40 per cent of the problem has been caused by salt contamination, that is why it is important to also re-plaster the walls with a salt-retardant plaster after insertion of a new damp-proof course.

to expose the brickwork so as to expose a dark or black-coloured strip running all along one horizontal course. At any rate, external soil should always be 150mm (6in) below interior floor levels, to allow for water evaporation outside. In some cases a French Drain (see Glossary) might be advisable. For reinstating a compromised DPC, one method is to inject silicone into one course of brickwork all around a building, then to apply waterproof plaster to a metre's height on the wall's inner face. However, installing a DPC in a building that never had one originally is considered by some experts to be ineffective. As mentioned above, it is also necessary to remove and replace internal plaster.

Condensation

What to Look For

Patches of ill-defined dampness on walls, presence of dark mould areas on walls behind furniture, musty smell, crescent-shaped areas of damp in an exposed corner. Visible droplets on shiny surfaces, e.g. tiles in an unventilated bathroom, window glass or a gloss-painted windowsill. Interstitial condensation is a potentially serious condition, whereby condensation that is trapped within a structure, usually after rising up through a permeable surface, cannot exit via roof, or other, ventilation. This can typically occur in a loft space, where moist air is allowed to enter from below.

Causes

Water vapour combines and travels with warm air, e.g. in the steam from a kettle or the vapour from hot water going into a bath. The concentration of the air's moisture is measured as its 'relative humidity'. As soon as the air cools below a certain temperature the moisture is separated from it, e.g. when kettle steam meets a cold tiled or glass surface, when droplets form. What is more, warm, moisture-laden air can swirl upwards and move considerable distances, e.g. from the bathroom to other rooms – usually rising higher as it travels, collecting in ceiling corners and behind furniture, where it becomes trapped, relinquishing its moisture on the wall's surface.

Cures

Install extractor fans in bathrooms and kitchens to remove warm moist air at source; you can buy fans that cut in when a certain level of humidity is reached. Try to increase ventilation and introduce low-level warmth throughout the house in winter. Install trickle vents near double-glazed windows,

Condensation within a room, droplets of water gathering on ceiling and walls. Property Care Association

Close-up of water droplets on ceiling, caused by condensation.
Property Care Association

ABOVE: **Bad mould in a corner: typical indications of a serious condensation problem.**
Property Care Association

RIGHT: **Close up of condensation in a bathroom, caused because there's no extractor fan.**

The condensation droplets on this window will inevitably lead to rot of the timber frame.

Damage and mould cause by dampness.
Property Care Association

Damage and mould caused by dampness.
Property Care Association

and fit air-bricks to outside walls, with an open/ close grill on the inside. To make the walls warmer, you can fill cavity wall cavities with insulating material. For a naturally humid area, e.g. a conservatory or swimming pool, you can use an electric dehumidifier unit, which extracts water from the air, and can be set to operate automatically above a specified humidity level. It is very important to remove mould growth: slightly sand down painted walls, then treat the surface with a fungicidal wash.

FLOODING

Five million properties in England and Wales are at risk of flooding, and places considered to be at risk from this danger are designated as being within a floodplain; when buying a house, this is one of the facts that should be established by your conveyancer or solicitor, and the risks assessed accordingly. The Environment Agency (EA) has a dedicated service called Floodline (0845 988 1188) and a website (www.envornment-agency.gov.uk), which you can contact to find out if your house is at risk, and this organization also issues free floodwarnings via Floodwarnings Direct (*see below*). From the EA website you can also ascertain if a property is in an area where there is a river or coastal flood risk, but this is a general guide only. You can also contact the National Flood Forum (01299 403055).

A property can be identified by the EA as being in an area where the risk of flooding is judged to be negligible, low, moderate or significant.

Prospective purchasers need to be aware that Flood Risk Surveys are not currently mandatory in the searches carried out for standard property searches. If your property is at significant risk of flooding, a suitably experienced chartered surveyor can carry out a detailed survey of it and report on the likely impact of a flood on the property, with recommendations as to any action that can be taken to reduce or eliminate these adverse effects, if a flood happens.

Flood risk reduces a building's value depending on the degree of risk of a flood happening or recurring, the severity of any previous flood and

---

Expert Quote

Chris Marsh, of Building Image, formerly with Hutton + Rostron Environmental Investigation Ltd:

Silicone damp-proof courses installed in buildings that never originally had a DPC, are not always effective, especially when used for very thick walls or ones with non-continuous mortar beds. It is impossible to guarantee the even distribution of the silicone material in this kind of wall. Also, there is no point in installing a DPC if the ground levels around the building are too high. These should be lowered, if necessary, first, and salts-damaged areas of plaster on the interior side of the walls must be replaced too.

Floodtite door shield. Floodtite Systems Ltd

the vulnerability of the property. A flood's impact can be reduced by increasing its flood resilience, i.e. its ability to withstand the effects of the water.

One consequence of a flood can be that the moistness does not dry out completely for a long time, especially in inaccessible places, such as under suspended ground floors. It is absolutely vital to thoroughly dry out all these voids and the timbers within them, otherwise rots inevitably develop in these concealed places over months if not years.

FLOODPLAIN

The Environment Agency (EA) uses this definition of a floodplain (copyright EA):

> This is defined as all land adjacent to a watercourse over which water flows in the time of flood, or would flow but for the presence of flood defences where they exist. The limits of floodplain are defined by the peak water level of an appropriate return period event on the watercourse or at the coast. On rivers this will normally be the greater of the 1-in-100 year return period or the highest known water level. In the coastal areas the 1-in-200 year flood or the highest new flood will be used, whichever is the greater. In both instances where a flood defence exists, which protects to a greater standard than those defined, then the floodplain is the area defended to the design water level.

If you are in a floodplain, the best plan is to prepare your house as much as you can. You cannot completely flood-proof a property but there are a number of things you can do to alter your home so as to minimize the subsequent damage. There are also a number of products you can install prior to flooding, which can then be activated as and when necessary.

Insurance

Insurance policies cover buildings and their contents damaged by major perils: wet perils, aircraft damage, fire, explosion, lightning, theft, earthquake and subsidence. Buildings' cover includes fixtures and fittings, terraces, footpaths, patios, swimming pools, tennis courts, drives, walls, fences, gates, hedges, sheds and greenhouses. If your home has to be rebuilt, you are covered for redecoration, storage and accommodation.

Check your buildings and contents insurance policies to see what cover they provide for flood damage. If you add changes that make the property more flood-resilient, tell your insurance company, as this might result in a reduction of your excess charges and/or your premiums. Whether you can get insurance cover obviously affects mortgage-ability. Insurance companies assess and grade flood risk in three bands: Band 1 means the risk is at up to 200:1 chance of an annual flood; Band 2 is between 200:1 and 75:1 chance annually; and Band 3 suggests a greater than 75:1 chance of an annual flood (very rare). These bands broadly correspond to the EA's assessment of low, moderate or significant categories.

Flood-risk cover and storm-damage cover are treated as separate risks for insurance purposes. From 2013, the Association of British Insurers (ABI) will no longer guarantee automatic flood-risk insurance to properties in Band 3, although this may be subject to review. Buildings insurance does not usually cover damage to outbuildings and gardens as a result of flooding, unless the policy conditions specifically state otherwise. The EA works with the ABI to support the insurance industry's commitment to continue offering flood risk insurance to the majority of homes in flood risk areas.

Are You Under-Insured?
You must make sure that your buildings insurance

covers the full cost of rebuilding the property. It is absolutely vital to realize that the cost of rebuilding may bear no relation to its market value. For instance, a listed building that needs specialist repairs done in a specific way could cost four times its market value to rebuild, and you have to be insured to cover this. Conversely, you might even save on premiums if you discover that rebuilding an ordinary house in a property hot spot could actually cost less than its saleable value. To ascertain the rebuild value of your house use the rebuilding cost table from the Royal Institution of Chartered Surveyors, or consult a suitably experienced surveyor for a valuation.

To get insurance cover if you live in a floodplain, get several quotes for flood cover. Contact the British Insurance Brokers Association (BIBA) for local insurance brokers. Insurance companies are offering flood cover based on actual risks of flooding in high-risk areas. Where permanent defences are not viable, they will want to know what other local flood-protection measures can be taken. They take account effective action people have taken to protect their homes, including the use of products approved by them, via the Kitemark scheme, where these reduce flood risk affecting those properties.

What to do Regarding Insurance
Claims for Flooding
Ask how long before the loss adjuster visits, and if you can clean the property or if they'll arrange someone to do this for you.

Make your own record of flood damage: use permanent ink pen to make marks on walls to indicate the height of floodwater in every room affected, and photograph or video damaged property, and list damage to property and buildings. Confirm that the insurance company will pay for any service or equipment you need, and make a note of all telephone calls, with the date, name of who you spoke to and precisely what has been agreed. Keep copies of all letters and emails you send and receive, keep receipts, and don't throw away anything until you have been told you can.

Flood Plan

This is a list of actions to take in the event of a flood, which you should prepare in advance:

Expert Quote

Robert Hooker, of the Subsidence Claims Advisory Bureau:

Some insurance companies are now declining to cover new policyholders in areas that have previously had flood claims. Some are asking for a flood-risk appraisal, which can cost as much as £500–£700, and even then there are no assurances that flood cover will be included. Bureau Insurance Services Ltd offers cover under their Flood Insure Scheme, where the risk is assessed on an individual basis and an on-site survey at a modest cost of £175 including VAT – details of this scheme can be found at: www.bureauinsure.co.uk.

---

1. Make arrangements for the eventuality of evacuation, obtain the contact details of the organizations concerned and keep these details to hand. If you have pets, find out if these are allowed at the evacuation centre and, if not, find a kennels or boarding facility.
2. Work out a list of things that you can move now, and move them: for instance, store mementos and personal items in a safe place.
3. Work out what you'll want to move: e.g. pets, cars, furniture, electrical equipment, garden pot-plants and furniture.
4. Check your insurance cover. Make sure you are covered properly (don't underestimate the value of your contents). Have contact numbers for the insurance company.
5. Find out how to turn off gas, electricity and water mains, and mark and label relevant switches and taps.
6. Gather together a flood kit (*see below*).
7. Find out how to use any flood defences you may have.
8. Obtain large polythene bags suitable for enclosing large goods and furniture that cannot be moved.

Flood-Warning Service

If you are registered with Floodline Warnings Direct (FWD), the EA's free flood-warning service,

Warnings and What to do at Each Stage

Flood watch: flooding is expected to roads and low lying land. Be alert for more warnings.

Flood alert: flooding is possible and you must be prepared. Be ready to act on your flood plan, gather together a flood kit, monitor local water levels on website.

Flood warning: a flood is expected and you must take immediate action. Move family pets and valuables to a safe place, keep your flood-kit ready, turn off gas, electricity and water supplies, and install your temporary flood-protection measures.

Severe flood warning: a severe flood is imminent, with danger to life or disruption to communities. Stay in a safe place with a means of escape, be ready to evacuate, cooperate with the emergency services and call 999 if you are in danger.

All clear: issued when flood watches or warnings are no longer in force.

Sources of Flooding

- Near a watercourse – such as a river, ditch, stream or open drain, when it cannot cope with the heavy rain. Fast-flowing floodwater can be a threat to safety and can damage buildings.
- Surface-water flooding, either run-off from hills or when rain overloads the area's drainage capacity. In the latter case, if drains are overloaded or get blocked, your house can get flooded with raw sewage.
- Coastal flooding: when waves or high water level goes over the defences.
- Groundwater flooding: when water levels in the ground rise above surface levels. This can occur separately or in combination with another source, e.g. surface flooding (surface and groundwater flooding account for 50 per cent of flooding).
- Reservoir flooding: a rare occurrence in which the water-containing 'dam' fails and a large amount of water is released very quickly.

Flood Facts

After a flood:

- 15cm (6in) of fast-flowing water can knock over an adult and a depth of 61cm (2ft) can move a car.
- Avoid walking or driving through flood-water.
- Keep children and vulnerable people away from the affected area.
- Wash your hands if you touch floodwater.
- It is vital to thoroughly dry out underfloor and concealed areas for a long time, otherwise rots can develop.
- Before turning on any mains' services, a qualified person must tell you they are safe to use.

General:

- Flood risk is not normally part of the standard search when you're buying a property.
- When buying flood-defence products, make sure they have the BSI kitemark.
- If floodwater is higher than 1m (3ft), it is better to allow it to enter your house, as its weight could damage walls.

you'll get flood alerts, warnings and severe flood warnings, plus messages telling you when these are no longer in force, at any time of day or night. Anyone registered for FWD messages gets any new flood alert messages. You get local information specific to your area; for instance, the time when flooding is expected, tide heights and affected locations, updated frequently. Contact Floodline to sign up on: 0845 988 1188 (or online).

How Water Gets Into Your House

Above Ground

It seeps through gaps and cracks around closed windows and doors; especially through the joints between frames and wall, as well as through cavities around pipes entering the property (e.g. for water, sewage, electricity, gas, vents for central heating systems, washing machines and tumble driers).

It can also come directly through the wall itself, either through permeable materials, or else through cracks or mortar joints, air-bricks, flues and vents, in addition to coming through a shared party wall from next door.

Below Ground

Water can seep through solid ground floors with no inherent damp-proof membrane, or which have a bad seal between floor and walls. It can also enter into the void below suspended ground floors, basements and cellars, through walls or floor, alternatively through cracks or gaps in the underground structure, e.g. gaps in foundations and basement walls. Water can also enter underground via a backflow cause by a blocked or overloaded sewage system.

Strategy for Long-Term Flood-Proofing of Your House

If your home is at risk of flooding there is a range of not-too-drastic measures you can take to alter your home, so that if/when a flood comes you can afterwards clean up quickly and easily, and there won't be long-term damage. If your home is listed, you may need Listed Building Consent for some of these – check with your local authority. And if your home is leasehold, you may need permission from the freeholder and/or other leaseholders. A chartered surveyor with experience in providing flooding-related services and advice will be able to give you individual advice and arrange the works. Some ideas are discussed below.

Walls

Install a second damp-proof course at a higher level. For cavity walls, fit a cavity-wall draining system. If

---

Key Actions Against Flooding

The EA advises the following key actions that you can take to protect against flooding:

- Go to the EA's website, check your flood risk and sign up for flood warnings.
- Raise electrical sockets and MCB control panels (fuse boxes) at least 1.5m (5ft) above the floor – do the same with TVs, stereos and electrical equipment.
- Fit water-resistant skirting boards, if possible – otherwise varnish wooden boards.
- Lay rugs over tiled floors rather than fit carpets.
- Install synthetic windows and doors – or varnish wooden ones.
- Fit non-return valves in vulnerable pipes.
- Where possible use water-resistant materials for fittings rather than wooden ones.
- Raise appliances such as fridges on to plinths.
- Check your insurance policy.

---

your house has waterproof render, or brick walls built using cement-based mortar, consider applying waterproof sealant on exterior walls and use water-resistant paint for internal decoration on the ground floor. However, if your house was built using water-permeable lime mortar, you must never attempt to waterproof either its walls' exterior or interior surfaces.

Consider fitting dry lining – that is a secondary wall in front of the main wall – with a cavity between that can be drained. Replace gypsum plaster using cement-based render or lime-based (not gypsum) plaster, because gypsum plaster does not resist water, and lime plaster is much more water-resistant.

Shelves

Fit high-mounted shelves on which to store valuable items.

Floors

If you have a concrete ground floor, make sure this is properly tanked (waterproofed). If it isn't, add

---

DIY Flood-Protection Items Needed

- Sandbags. Contact a local builders' merchants, alternatively ask your local authority.
- Sheets of plywood/nails, for makeshift blocking of entry points.
- Plastic sheeting.
- Bricks, blocks of timber.
- Hand tools: hammer, saw, etc.

a damp-proof membrane (DPM – thick builders' polythene), either by placing it on the top surface and adding an extra screed on top of it, or by digging up the current screeding, installing the DPM and re-laying a screed. Lay tiles over concrete floors and use rugs rather than carpets. If you have timber, tiled or flagstone ground floors, replace them with solid or suspended concrete floors with good DPMs within. Use water-resistant finishes such as tiled flooring over concrete. Incorporate a slight fall in the floor and install a sump pump to ground or basement floors to remove any floodwater.

Doors/Windows

If possible, raise door thresholds and/or buy purpose-built floodboards that can be installed immediately prior to flooding (*see below*). Fit waterproof windows and doors of either plastic or metal; failing this, paint or varnish wooden windows. Fit internal doors that can easily be removed. Patio doors should ideally be replaced with windows or ordinary doors made from plastic or varnished materials.

Air-Bricks

Get specially designed covers that fit over the holes of ventilation bricks or grills.

Drains and Pipes

Install backflow valves on sanitary drains to prevent upsurge of sewage. Fit non-return valves to water outlet and inlet pipes.

Services

Increase the height of MCB boxes (or fuse boxes), meter and company fuse, as well as electrical sockets to a minimum of 1.5m (5ft) above floor level. Ideally replace wiring that runs under the ground floor, and run the cables down the wall from above. Raise the height of gas intakes and meter and piping to this same height.

Skirting Boards

Replace yours with water-resistant skirting boards.

Electrical Appliances

To save moving HiFi, computers, TVs, etc. prior to a flood, consider fixing them on shelves or brackets to the wall, higher than 1.5m (5ft) above floor level.

Chipboard

This material is used for most kitchen and some bathroom cabinets, and fragments upon extensive soaking. If possible, replace units made from this material with ones made from solid wood, plastic or stainless steel.

Install a Pump

If you have a basement or void under the ground floor, consider fitting a pump, to remove floodwater after the event.

Valuable Items

Store these on shelves at a high level.

Plumbing/Air-Conditioning

Ideally the boiler, hot-water cylinder, air-conditioning units and heating and ventilation components should be put on the first floor or in the loft. However, metal radiators and pipes are unlikely to be adversely affected.

Kitchen/Bathroom

Use water-resistant materials, e.g. stainless steel, plastic or real wood instead of chipboard. Raise fridges and appliances on plinths, if practical.

Flood-Proofing Products You Can Buy

When planning what products to get, bear in mind that you have to consider the pressure of water above ground level and also seepage below ground level. There is a comprehensive list of these in the 'Blue Pages' directory on the National Flood Forum's website (www.floodforum.org.uk). Always check that a product has been tested and displays the BSI kitemark or equivalent accreditation for national quality standard PAS 1188. The British Standard Institution has a list of manufacturers of these products online (www.kitemark.com). Also the Flood Protection Association has lists of these (www.floodprotectionassoc.co.uk).

Sandbags

Either buy these ready-filled or get empty bags and the sand from DIY stores, builders' merchants or your local authority. Don't fill bags more than half full and there is no need to tie the end of the bag. Remove debris from where they are to be placed. Place half-filled bags lengthways and parallel to the direction of water's flow. Tuck the opened end under the filled part. Place them in layers like a brick wall, staggering the joints. Stamp on bags to eliminate gaps and create a seal. If your wall is more than two sandbags high, it should have a double line of sandbags at the bottom, followed by a second double line, then a single line on top.

Flood Sacks

A lighter, modern version of sandbags. They need to be soaked in water so they expand, then placed around entrances to your home. If they have not been in contact with contaminated water, they can afterwards be left to dry and shrink and can be reused.

Temporary Freestanding Barriers

These are units that fit together to create a kind of artificial wall some distance from a property or properties, in order to hold back or deflect floodwater. They can either be rigid or flexible, and some use a separate frame to support the barrier, and might be comprised of an air- or water-filled tube.

In addition to blocking water, their aim is to reduce the seepage of groundwater into the lower foundations and ground-floor level. A pump is normally installed within the 'dry' area in order to dispose of any water that slips through.

Flood Boards/Door Guards or Barriers

For doors these are usually a metal or plastic floodboard that can be installed to block water's entry underneath; they normally slide into a frame attached to the door or window frame, so as to form a watertight seal.

Air-Brick Covers

These take the form of plastic boxes with a permanent frame screwed to the wall, and a cover that clips against them. Can be fitted over air-bricks or wall vents.

Flood Skirts

These are designed to be fixed all around the property to prevent water's ingress through the building fabric, as well as openings.

Air-brick cover. Floodtite Systems Ltd

Large Sealable Bags

You can buy extra-large sealable polythene bags to protect items that are hard to move, such as sofas.

Pump

Fit one in the basement or underfloor area.

Costs

These depend on the size of the property and severity of flooding you need to protect against. According to the ABI, to protect against shallow flash floods it costs between £2,000 and £6,000, and to safeguard against prolonged flooding £20,000 to £40,000. There is also Property Level Flood Protection Funding to some local authorities and local EA teams to undertake flood surveys of properties in high-risk areas, where provision and installation of household flood protection measures may also be funded.

Practical Steps to Take in the Event of a Flood

As soon as Floodline give you an advance warning, take the following steps. If possible, drive your car to higher ground, especially if it's housed in a garage. Make sure you know where your pets are – take them to another location or kennels' boarding service unless the evacuation centre accepts pets (check on this). Move any large or loose items or weight them down.

Checklist – Inside

1. Turn off gas, electricity and water supplies. Disconnect cooker, dishwasher and washing machine from water and drains, then block

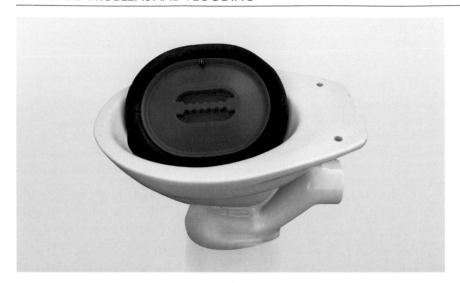

Panseal, special device for blocking up a WC prior to a flood, to prevent backflow.
Floodtite Systems Ltd

holes to open drainpipes thus revealed, using cloth or rags rammed in. If you have a gas cooker with a bayonet fitting that you can easily disconnect, do so.

2. Unplug all electrical appliances and take upstairs any that you can.
3. Move as much furniture and electrical appliances upstairs as you are able.
4. Remove all items from cupboards, furniture and so on, and take these upstairs, including drawers.
5. Take upstairs all personal items, bank and insurance details, papers, jewellery, phones and so on.
6. If possible roll up carpets and rugs and take them upstairs.
7. Using sandbags, put weighted plugs into sinks and baths, and also sandbag toilet bowls.
8. Move all kitchen chemicals, food and so on up to higher levels.
9. Remove upstairs all remaining movable items.
10. Ideally remove internal doors and take them upstairs, or prop them open. Take down curtains, or hang them over rods out of the way of water.
11. Raise heavy furniture and appliances up on bricks, and move them away from the wall. Weight down unmovable furniture.
12. If practical, apply silicone sealant around the inside of open ground-floor doors and window frames, then close them.

Checklist – Outside
1. Assess all entry points for water. Using DIY items or flood-protection products try to block these as efficiently as you can, using sandbags, plastic sheeting, etc. Never install protective barriers that are higher than 1m (3ft) high, because above this height it is safer to let water into the house: at higher levels than this the weight of water could do irreparable damage.
2. Move dustbins and the contents of sheds and garages elsewhere.
3. Weigh down manhole covers with sandbags.
4. Cut off the flow from propane tanks and/or oil drums.
5. Work with neighbours to make measures effective – particularly important if you are in a terrace or semi-detached house, because water can come through the walls.

Checklist – Afterwards
1. When the rain has stopped, contact your insurance company, then Floodline to confirm that the danger has passed. Take photos or a video as evidence for your insurance claim. Don't dispose of any items you're claiming for until this has been authorized by your insurance company – you may need the damaged item as evidence.
2. Remember that floodwater might be contaminated. Open manholes, broken glass and items that can trip you up can be invisible.

3. Prior to cleaning up, put on protective clothes, boots, gloves and a face mask and get a tetanus injection if yours is out of date. Clean and cover any cuts and grazes.

4. Do not enter fast-flowing water.

5. If the electricity supply is not already switched off at the main, get a qualified person to do this. NB: Do not touch sources of electricity when standing in floodwater.

6. Be prepared to face vermin that may have taken shelter in your home.

7. Remove standing water with a generator-driven pump, or the fire brigade may offer this service. Only pump out water when the flood levels outside your property start to be lower than those inside – this reduces the risk of structural damage.

8. Shovel mud away evenly from both sides of a wall – this stops pressure building up on one side.

9. If you are using a dehumidifier, keep doors and window closed, if not keep them open.

10. Get rid of mud and hose down surfaces and dispose of the debris. Scrub all surfaces with hot soapy water, disinfect food-preparation areas.

11. Remove coverings from air-bricks and vents and open windows and doors.

12. Have gas, electricity and water supplies and your boiler checked for safety by qualified people (Gas Safe register for gas, NICEIC or ECA-registered for electricity) before you use them.

13. If your central heating system has been passed as safe to use, switch it on. Otherwise use industrial portable heaters to dry things out. Hire a dehumidifier and use it to extract moisture from the air as things dry out.

14. Check that the waste-water runs freely down the sewer. Private sewage systems should not be used until water in the surrounding field is lower than the water level around the property. After flooding, damaged septic tanks, cesspools and small-package sewage systems should be serviced and inspected as soon as possible by a professional person.

15. Do not start major repair work until your insurance company has approved this. Also, if you are making an insurance claim, don't dispose of any item that's to be replaced until you're told to do so by the insurer.

16. Electrical appliances exposed to flooding should be checked by a qualified person before they are used.

17. Run taps for a short time to check silt has not entered the system – if you suspect contamination, contact your water company.

18. Water supplies from wells and cisterns may be contaminated and should not be used until tested for safety.

19. If you have suspended timber ground-floors, lift some boards to see when the water has drained away and leave the area open for a long time so that the timber can fully dry out.

20. If practical, remove vinyl wallpapers, gloss paint and tiling from walls to allow drying out.

21. Don't redecorate for at least three months after the walls have dried out.

22. Kitchen chipboard units made of chipboard are likely to be irrevocably damaged, so you're likely to need to replace these.

Structural Damage

Signs to look for afterwards are:

- Buckling of walls, horizontal cracking or areas that seem to have moved out of vertical alignment.
- Vertical or diagonal cracks, which may indicate that walls or footings are affected.
- Bulging or dislodged sections.
- Deep scouring that has led to exposed foundations.
- Any new cracks bigger than 5mm (¼in) above doors and windows.
- Changes in the line or appearance of the roof ridge.

If you see any of the above, contact your insurance company and consult a chartered surveyor or structural engineer.

CHAPTER 7

DIY Disasters and Sundry Problems

UNDOING MAJOR BOTCHED JOBS THAT NEED URGENT ATTENTION

Homeowners and inept builders can make terrible, sometimes irreparable, mistakes. Here are some examples of some major and not so major botched jobs, and the best approaches to sorting them out. The method of undoing the disasters is described, to show how professionals would tackle the work or, alternatively, for smaller jobs, ways you might be able to do it yourself.

Amateur Loft-Conversion

Vital, supportive roof joists are likely to have been removed. What's more, furniture and the weight of people walking are added to timbers that were intended only to support a ceiling. This can result in roof sag or collapse, as well as bulging walls, this being caused because they are moving outwards. Building regulation approval for a loft-conversion is mandatory and only given if fire safety regulations are met and the structural support is correct. Professional loft-convertors have to build extra walls and incorporate additional supports to ensure that the loft room's floor is adequate and that the roof is properly supported. Check with the local authority (LA) to find out if building regulations' approval has been granted.

Signs to Look For
Foreshortened stumps of cut-off joists, sagging ceilings and/or bulging walls and/or a sagging roof. To judge whether the loft-conversion has been done properly, look at the floor's cross-section though the stairwell. If the combined floor and ceiling thickness is under 17–20cm (7–8in), the chances are that the installers have put the loft's floor on the existing ceiling joists, and have not put in proper flooring joists. The correct procedure is for new loft-floor joists to be installed, which have the requisite support beneath and adequate provision for supporting the roof, normally supplied by newly created supportive masonry, called a 'dwarf' wall. There should always be an entrance lobby and a suitable stairway with a fire door either at the top of the bottom of this.

What to Do
Consult a structural engineer urgently, in order to devise a strategy to reintroduce support to the roof, or alternatively go to a loft-conversion company for a new, legal, conversion job to be carried out.

Removal of Load-Bearing Walls

These particular structures support the floor(s) above, so their removal can cause sagging of the floor or even collapse. In some Georgian houses, even thin timber partition walls may provide necessary support.

Signs to Look For
Ridges on the floor and/or lines on the ceiling suggesting evidence of a wall's presence, and visible building movement.

What to Do
Consult a structural engineer, who may recommend the insertion of horizontal supports or rebuilding of the wall.

Chimney-Breast Removed, Without Supporting the Stack Above

When an older house was built with chimneys, the rectangular breasts were built up from downstairs to upstairs rooms, then on to the chimney-stack above, as one complete unit. If either or both of the breasts are removed, then the heavy stack above is unsupported and could crash down into the house. When a chimney-breast has been removed correctly, the brickwork is slanted at an angle beneath the breast above, indicating that there's adequate support. If the breast has been cut off square, it indicates a dangerous amateur botch.

Signs to Look For

Part of a chimney-breast evident, cut squarely off, indications of cracks and movement of the brickwork.

What to Do

Consult a structural engineer for advice.

Roof Sag Caused by (Heavier) Concrete Tiles Being Used to Replace Clay or Slate

Roof joists are designed to support a specific weight of roof tile, so if your original roof was of slate and this has been replaced by concrete or clay tiles, the extra weight can cause the timbers to warp, bend or break.

Signs to Look For

The roof sagging, bowing or the roof-support timber in the loft bowing or becoming warped.

What to Do

Consult a structural engineer, who may recommend additional support to the beams or renewal or replacement of tiles with the lighter ones.

This stone-clad house looks fine, but being semi-detached it does not match the neighbour's property.

BOTCHES YOU CAN LIVE WITH FOR A WHILE BUT NEED ADDRESSING ASAP

Stone-Cladding on a Brick Wall

Aside from looking inappropriate, some impervious stone surfaces prevent brick from naturally relinquishing rainwater to the atmosphere. Therefore, moisture is locked within the masonry, creating damp problems or brick cracking when the liquid freezes. Some local authorities require you to get planning permission for stone-cladding, particularly in conservation areas. You could, therefore, have an enforcement action taken against you to remove it, even if it was put there by a previous owner.

The cladding panels are usually of 'cast stone' (a form of concrete, whereby stone powder, sand and white cement is mixed and cast into moulds). These are bonded to the brickwork using resin glues that are stronger than the masonry, which means the brick outer surface will be ravaged when cladding is chipped away, what's more it's a very labour-intensive process – using a mechanical demolition hammer (kango) to power a masonry chisel. Afterwards you may need to have bricks replaced, or possibly the wall might have to be rebuilt.

Painted Brickwork or Pointing, When Incorrect Paint Has Been Used

Brick walls move continually due to changing heat and moisture content, and this causes the wrong sort of paint layer on the surface to split. Good-quality masonry paint, or the type of applied finish that is sprayed on professionally, is specially formulated so as to be elastic enough to move with the masonry and not crack. But if the wrong sort of paint is used and its surface cracks, moisture creeps behind the painted area, which blows off even more paint in localized areas. What's worse is that the remaining paint can adhere very well and is hard to remove without damaging the bricks' outer surface – this brick 'fireskin' is extremely

ABOVE: **Neglected woodwork will lead to rotten timber.**

LEFT: **The wrong paint was used on this masonry, now it looks dreadful.**

Close-up to show how paint comes off in patches if either the wrong paint was used or the surface was not properly prepared.

ABOVE: **The wrong type of paint was used on this wall.**

BELOW: **The wrong type of paint was used on this kitchen wall.**

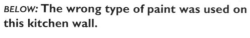

Peeling paint.

How a painted house should look – an excellent and professional surface finish applied to a grand Edwardian house. John Moore, Specialist Resins

important, and provides a measure of waterproofing that stops the bricks absorbing water. Because using a blowlamp or abrasive-blasting methods is likely to damage the brickwork, chemical paint-removers work best. This is a very messy and potentially hazardous job, definitely for a specialist. For stripping paint from pointing, this again requires a chemical paint-remover.

Inappropriate Windows

In a conservation area you need permission to replace windows with a different type, and you are liable to replace examples that contravene the rules. Most Edwardian and Victorian facades need authentic period windows to maintain their market value. Period-style double-glazed sash windows are available from several companies, such as Ventrolla. The National Conservatory Advisory Service and the National Replacement Window

Advisory Service, (www.nrwas.org; 0800 028 5809) can provide advice and access to the best products, manufacturers and locally based tradespeople throughout England.

Illegally Built Extension

Any extension larger than a certain size requires planning permission from the local authority, and any extension needs to comply with building control regulations. From a practical point of view, if it has been built without approval from your local building control department, it could collapse, or not be watertight, have insufficient foundations or not be bonded to the main structure, and is unlikely to be properly insulated. What's more, lack of official building control approval and/or planning permission (if needed) are likely to blight any future sale.

Signs to Look For

Cracking, perhaps apparent movement, lack of any record of local authority permission being granted, or building control approval. If in doubt consult the LA, and they will have records of whether permission/approval has been granted or not.

What to Do

Tell the LA and ask if you can apply for retrospective planning permission and building control approval. This may be forthcoming, even if partial rebuilding is stipulated. Worst case scenario is that they may insist it is demolished.

Extremely Damp Cellar

Unless they are professionally damp-proofed, cellars are usually slightly damp, but when plaster and decorations soon blister and decay and there's a great deal of mould and mildew, the problems need addressing. By its nature, most of a cellar is likely to be below the water table, so the situation is managed in one of two ways. 'Tanking' – meaning totally waterproofing – of the walls, done professionally, utilizes the application of a special waterproofing material and extreme attention to detail: afterwards it's vital that the material is not punctured by nails or screws. The other approach is called 'dry lining', where a dimple-backed membrane is fixed to the wall and another wall is built against this membrane. The dimples then allow space for

water behind the topmost wall to run down the walls to the base, and the water is pumped from here, the pump being activated automatically in the presence of water. Taking this principle further, a new wall may be built in front of the old, leaving a cavity for water to drain into, this procedure is termed 'dry lining'.

PROBLEMS WHICH AN EXPERIENCED HANDYMAN MAY BE ABLE TO TACKLE

Marked as either cosmetic only or urgent.

Non-Matching or Unsuitable Pointing (Urgent)

Typically this is where hard, cement-based mortars are used to point walls where the mortar was lime-based, and consequently soft. Because the hard cement-based material repels water to a marked degree, this water is driven into the bricks, eventually causing dampness or brick decay. The pointing mortar should always match the original, meaning that for a pre-1850 house (if built using lime mortar, not cement) the mortar mix should use lime as a binder. Chip out the incorrect mortar using a plugging, or cold chisel: do not use an angle grinder or power tool as this will damage the adjacent bricks. Always carefully match the colour, texture and strength of pointing mortars. Cement mortars are reasonably straightforward to match; however, lime mortars can be analysed by specialist firms such as Anglia Lime (see Contacts). You can send them a sample and they can tell you what sand to use and what proportion to mix it with lime. Joint finishes must match rest of the building (see Chapter 9).

Non-Matching Rendering (Urgent)

This can be removed using a heavy club hammer and sharp masonry chisel, or an electric demolition hammer (kango) operating a chisel tip. Rendering may come away in large sheets leaving a good surface, but if it has bonded well the stone or brick may be irrevocably damaged.

Textured Ceilings (Cosmetic Only, Unless Damaged and Crumbling)

Early (pre-1985) 'Artex' texturing material contained a small proportion of asbestos, so in view of this, if it is in good condition it's best to leave it alone (see below). This material has been asbestos-free since the mid-1980s and now Artex Bluehawk make a plaster material designed to be applied to the textured surface, that can fill in the depressions to create a smooth finish. If an old Artex-coated ceiling has become crumbly or broken it could represent a health hazard, and only a registered asbestos contractor should handle it: approach your local environmental health officer in the first instance for advice.

A textured ceiling can also be 'overnailed', meaning nailing plasterboard to it, using long nails, after which a plasterer applies a skim coating of plaster to smooth it off.

NB: The joists need to be robust enough to take the extra weight; and the presence of a cornice might make this impossible.

Polystyrene Ceiling Tiles (Cosmetic, But There May be Safety Issues)

Use of these has been banned in kitchens because of the highly toxic fumes they release on combustion. It is easy to knock them off with a paint scraper but you'll be left with five 'dabs' of hard adhesive. You might be able to remove these with a paint scraper, alternatively a sharp carpenter's chisel or else a chemical stripper. Be aware that pieces of plaster may pull from the ceiling, attached to the tiles. In this case you may be able to make patch repairs, using 'fine filler' type material, or alternatively fix another plasterboard ceiling beneath it (as above, ceiling joists must be able to support the extra weight).

Painted Ceilings and Ceiling Beams (Cosmetic)

Painted cornices and ceiling centres often have paint-clogged decorative crevices, adversely affecting the appearance. Chemical strippers, the 'poultice' type, where the paint is drawn into a putty-like material, is the answer. For painted timber, black gloss paint looks brash on ancient oak. Using a power sander always leaves scratch marks on the beautiful historic wood, so the only answer is to use chemical stripper.

Blocked Air-Bricks (Urgent)

Ventilation is vital beneath suspended timber ground-floors, so that dampness and stale air, which encourage wood rot, can be dissipated. Similarly the roof space, at eaves level, needs ventilation. Air-bricks are either bricks incorporating rows of holes, or an iron plate with a grill of holes, set into the brickwork. Air-bricks, necessarily just above ground level, are often blocked by soil, debris or sometimes paving slabs or a patio are laid that blocks the holes. Clear away all obstructions.

Bridged Damp-Proof Course (DPC) (Urgent) Structurally Important

A DPC is an impervious layer of slates, bituminized felt or lead, laid between brick courses to stop water and salts rising up the wall from the ground. These were not mandatory until around 1880, prior to which it was accepted that walls would absorb and then relinquish water (see Chapter 6). It's very important that, if present, the DPC must not have anything (e.g. soil, patio or slabs) covering it, as this allows water to 'bridge' across it and up the wall. Rendering should not cover a DPC, as this causes the same effect: rendering should stop above and below the DPC – if your wall rendering is painted, you may not be able to see the DPC, but it may well be perfectly functional. Treatment is removal of the bridging element.

Weakened Floor Joist(s) (Structurally Necessary)

This can occur when the timber is cut too deeply to accommodate pipes and/or cables. Treatment is replacement of the joist; however, a structural engineer may suggest ways of strengthening, rather than replacing, it. Replacing the joist may necessitate removing all the floorboards in the room, and possibly inserting joist ends into cavities in the wall, so it is to be avoided if possible.

Rotting or Incorrectly Laid, Timber Floating Floor (Cosmetic)

A 'floating' timber floor is so-called because it's completely bonded horizontally but not to the subfloor, on top of which it rests; this is in contrast to floorboards, which are nailed separately to joists. If a floating floor is laid on to concrete that has no damp-proof membrane, moisture will rise and rot the timber. Replace the floor, first installing a layer of thick builder's polythene beneath, in addition to the foam cushioning layer. A squeaky timber floating floor, or one with ridges and raised areas, is likely not to have an expansion gap around the edge, which is vital, or else may not have the foam cushioning underneath – the solution is to remove and relay it properly.

Gypsum-Based Plaster and Plasterboard Used to Reinstate Parts of Lime-Based Plastered Area (Cosmetic)

Lime plaster is difficult to use, so repairs to it may have been done using readily available gypsum plaster. However, the materials are incompatible and tend to crack at their juncture. The only repair is to hack away the wrong material and redo the repair using lime-based plaster. Using lime plaster is a very skilled job, so enlist the help of a professional.

Quarry Tiled or Tessellated Floor That's Covered Up (Cosmetic)

Sometimes attractive period features like this were covered by a concrete screed. All you can do is carefully break up the screed and hope that the surface beneath has not been ruined. However, in some old cottages, paving slabs were laid straight on to the soil. In such a case, groundwater will obviously rise through these unless a damp-proof membrane is applied to prevent it. So, if you remove old floor coverings and come across a black bitumen layer or polythene, take advice on how to replace it, if you need to.

Pine-Cladding

Use a sharp chisel to prize up boards at the end or edge, then slide a large screwdriver behind to lever off the cladding planks, inserting it as close to the nail positions as you can get. Nail holes may not show, but can be filled if they do.

CHIMNEY PROBLEMS

Building regulations now require that all new chimneys need to have a flue lining. This was not true in the past, when a weak mortar called 'parging' was used, which can often decay, leaving the chimney working inefficiently.

Blockages

Chimneys need regular sweeping, otherwise fires will smoke dangerously, what's more you can have a chimney fire, where collected debris stuck in the chimney catches alight. A rudimentary test for blockages is to light a spill of paper and hold it in the fireplace. If the flame is drawn upwards, this indicates there are no blockages. If the flame stays still it could indicate that there is one. For blockages, professionals use a Coring Ball (a heavy weight on a chin) to remove them, or else an automatically self-centring Power Reaming Device.

Checklist of Warning Signs

- Windows out of keeping with nearby houses.
- Stone-cladding on brickwork.
- Painted brickwork.
- Illegal loft-conversion.
- Any sign of distortion in the building, particularly indicated by sticking doors.
- Visible sagging of the roof.
- Obvious structural changes, such as apparently missing wall.
- Newly built extensions or conservatories – check they have permission/ building regulation approval.
- Large cracks in walls, inside or outside, or any evidence of such cracks being recently filled.

Leaks

If you think your chimney may have cracks or leaks you can have a CCTV survey. If a chimney leaks because of the erosion of stone or brick, you can have this repaired from the outside by repointing with weak mortar. Alternatively, you can have the chimney relined with a refractory concrete or a metallic liner. Smoke blowing back into the room can be caused by a chimney with the wrong flue size, leaks, air starvation, partial blockage, as well as other things. If the chimney-breast feels hot, this is an indication that the chimney may have deteriorated. Stains on the breast show that tar or acids have condensed inside the flue and are corroding the masonry.

Leaning or Unstable Chimney

This is caused by erosion, acid attack or the breakdown of the chimney bricks' bonding mortar. You either have to have the chimney rebuilt, using the same bricks and matching mortar or, if the chimney is not needed, have it demolished and tile over the gap: high winds could dislodge part of it, and its collapse would be likely to smash anything below it, or even kill or injure someone.

Relining

The 'parging' lining inside an old chimney is liable to break down. The solution is to have it relined.

Flashing Failure

At the junction between the roof and the emerging chimney, the lead flashing or mortar flaunching often breaks down and needs professional attention to stop leaking. If you don't need the chimney, you can simply dismantle it, as above.

Damp Transferred to Interior Rooms

A redundant chimney needs to be capped off to block out rainwater, but this has to be done in such a way so as to permit ventilation.

Trade Federations with Lists of Their Members in Your Area on their Websites

National Association of Chimney Sweeps (NACS) (www.chimneyworks.co.uk; 01785 811732). This professional trade association promotes high standards for the sweeping, inspection and maintenance of chimneys. Members work to the NACS code of practice and code of conduct. It also encompasses chimney engineers, who can maintain appliances, install flue systems, stainless-steel flexible liners and flue terminations.

National Association of Chimney Engineers (NACE) (www.nace.org.uk; 0800 0924019). A register of competent chimney engineers for all types of chimney work. NACE-approved chimney-lining installers provide an economic solution to all problems relating to damaged flueways by giving an alternative to demolishing and rebuilding the stack itself. They can give advice as to the type of lining required to suit the appliance and make sure that it conforms to the statutory building regulations and manufacturer's recommendations.

HEATING APPLIANCES/ STOVES/CHIMNEY FITTING

All such items must be fitted by a competent person, and the official body that authorizes and registers installers is HETAS Ltd (www.hetas.co.uk; 0845 634 5626), which is the official body recognized by the government to approve biomass and solid-fuel domestic heating appliances, fuels and services, including the registration of competent installers and servicing business.

HETAS Services Key Points

- This is the only government-approved competent-persons scheme specializing in solid fuel, wood and biomass.
- All registered installers are trained and regularly assessed as competent.
- The HETAS scheme covers a range of installations that an installer may carry out: dry appliances, appliances with boilers, solid mineral, wood and biomass appliances, hot water and heating systems along with re-lining chimneys.
- HETAS is the official body for testing and approval of appliances and publishes lists of approved appliances, fuels and equipment to help consumers, installers, retailers, designers and specifiers in choosing an installation and system to suit your needs, while complying

with the relevant building regulations and safety standards.

What You Need to Know

The information in the box below is courtesy of Chimney Fit Installation Service, who manufacture chimney-fitting items, with special thanks to Allister Moorcroft, of that company (www.chimneyfit. co.uk).

ASBESTOS

This material had so many useful qualities that it was used as a building material until the 1980s but has now been completely outlawed, and its presence is always noted on surveyors' reports. The overriding rule is that asbestos materials that are in good condition are safe unless its fibres become airborne, something that can happen when it is damaged, sanded or drilled, for which reason these actions are proscribed. Tampering with asbestos in any form is to be avoided for health reasons, you cannot dispose of it at an ordinary council waste premises, and if you have certain asbestos products in your home and want to remove them, you have to employ a specialist contractor, who has the knowledge and equipment to remove the material and dispose of it in a safe way.

Important Things You Need To Know

(Copyright, Chimney Fit Installation Service.)

- A combustion appliance is a controlled item under the building regulations.
- Planning permission is required, unless you use an approved installer.
- You must install a carbon monoxide alarm with every new solid fuel appliance.
- Appliances must meet the efficiencies as laid done in the Domestic Heating Compliance Guide.
- Under new guidelines you require a commissioning plan.
- Unless your chimney is installed to manufacturers' recommendations they will not warranty their chimney.
- You are responsible for the safety of installers working at height.

A specialist asbestos removal contractor wears fully protective clothing and breathing apparatus, and will seal off the working area before spraying any friable material with solutions to seal its surface, termed encapsulation. Special suction machines remove all dust and the material is dismantled and put into marked containers or bags before being taken away. Afterwards independent analysts carry out tests to make sure that no fibres remain.

What are the Risks to Health?

Asbestos fibres are naturally present in the environment, and everyone is already exposed to very low levels of these, at no apparent harm. But tradespeople who have worked with the material are particularly at risk because they may have inhaled the fibres at high concentrations. The diseases that result are mesothelioma, asbestosis, lung cancer and diffuse pleural thickening. These very serious illnesses usually occur many years after the initial exposure to the material. The Health and Safety Executive (HSE) state that a key risk factor in the risk of developing an asbestos-related disease is the total number of fibres breathed in. Working on or near damaged asbestos-containing materials or breathing in high levels of asbestos fibres, which may be many hundreds of times that of environmental levels, can increase your chances of getting an asbestos-related disease. If you want to know precisely which asbestos materials you can safely have contact with, and what precautions to take when doing so, the HSE produce task sheets can help (http://www.hse.gov.uk/absestos/essentials/index.htm).

Asbestos-Containing Materials Used in Buildings

Asbestos Cement

This is a hard grey material, typically containing 10–15 per cent asbestos. It is used to make asbestos cement roofs (typically in corrugated sheeting) often on garage roofs or of sheds – they often attract growths of moss. It is less commonly used to make asbestos wall-cladding, typically of a building with an asbestos roof, to make downpipes and gutters (normally in industrial buildings), and asbestos cement flues, in boiler systems, air-conditioning and ventilation systems. The material's hardness

Corrugated asbestos cement roof in a garage – see how moss grows all over it.

means it's less likely to become friable and release fibres, meaning it's safer than most other forms of the material, unless used in combination with other asbestos products, such as certain asbestos coatings.

Textured Finishes on Ceilings and Walls
(3½–4½ per cent asbestos)
Applied to give a stippled, or textured finish. Artex was (and is) one of the most well-known. The fibres are locked into place and only pose a threat if these surfaces are sanded down. It was some-

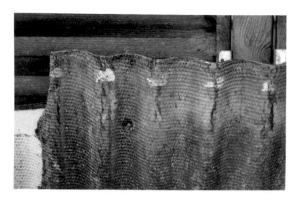

times applied on to other asbestos materials, such as asbestos insulating board.

Floor Tiles
Asbestos floor tiles have a low percentage of asbestos and might be hidden under carpets; the material was sometimes used to make vinyl floor tiles.

Asbestos Composites
Contains 25–40 per cent asbestos and is found typically in the bathroom as bath side-panels, airing cupboard linings, window sills and toilet cisterns and seats.

Textiles
Old fire blankets and heat-resistant gloves, and behind old fuse boxes.

Paper
For lining under tiles and inside metal cladding.

Close up of a sheet of corrugated asbestos cement.

Asbestos-Containing Building Materials That You are Advised Not to Handle Under Any Circumstances Unless You are an HSE-Licensed Contractor

Sprayed Coatings
Insulation that was applied to the underside of roofs and the sides of industrial buildings, as well as on steel and reinforced concrete beams and columns and the underside of floors. Coloured white or grey (or it may be painted), it has a rough surface and contains 85 per cent asbestos.

Asbestos Insulating Board (AIB)
(25–40 per cent asbestos)
Fireproofing panels in fire doors, lift-shaft linings, ceiling tiles, soffits, panels below windows and partition walls.

Lagging and Insulation
This is a fibrous material that flakes and powders easily, and can be found on heating systems, for instance around boilers or calorifiers and pipework. It may be covered in a protective coating or painted. One of the most dangerous asbestos materials known.

Loose-Fill Asbestos
A loose, fluffy material that can be blue-grey or white in colour. It is used for insulating houses and industrial buildings, and can also be found between cavity walls, under floorboards and in loft spaces.

Asbestos Facts

- Asbestos products can be hard to identify. If in doubt, consult your local environmental health officer, who can advise you.
- If you think you have asbestos dust in your home, e.g. coming from pipe lagging, don't suck it up with a vacuum cleaner, as the fibres are too small to be trapped and will be spread throughout the air.
- Never prod or poke friable matter that you suspect could be an asbestos product.
- Never use power tools or sandpaper or a brush on any material you suspect may contain an asbestos product.
- Do not break up asbestos cement products or asbestos boards, as this releases dust.
- It is illegal to mix asbestos products with your household waste, or to take it to your council recycling centre, unless your local authority have advised you of the correct recycling centre to take it to: they will stipulate how it is to be bagged up.
- If you're considering buying a property where there is asbestos material that is deemed to be harmful, get a quote from a licensed operator for its removal, and use this quote to bargain the price down. Alternatively, make the sale dependent on the removal of the asbestos.

CHAPTER 8

Rots and Infestations

WOOD ROTS

What are Wood Rots?

Wood can be attacked by a range of fungi that extract nutrients, effectively feeding on it. In order to survive, both wet and dry rots always require an external source of fresh water and thrive in stagnant, unventilated areas, typically in cellars, under suspended timber floors or loft spaces under leaky roofs, or sometimes in timber within damp walls. There are a variety of so-called 'brown' rots and 'white' rots with various Latin names, but for practicality they are usually divided into dry rot, which is one specific fungus called *Serpula lacrymans*, and all the other rots,

collectively known as wet rots, which do not spread so quickly and are comparatively easy to eradicate. Dry rot, however, spreads quickly and is difficult to destroy.

Wet rots require damper conditions than dry rot, and treatment is a question of stopping the ingress of water, introducing ventilation, and replacing the rotten timber with preservative-treated wood. An outbreak of wet rot can sometimes send strands (hypha) across brickwork (notably cellar fungus) in search of more timber, but provided a professional precludes dry rot, masonry-protective measures are not usually needed once the original outbreak and cause is removed.

Close shot of an outbreak of dry rot. Warren Woodworm Ltd and Waverley Building Preservation Ltd

Here, dry rot has completely covered underfloor timber joists. Warren Woodworm Ltd and Waverley Building Preservation Ltd

Dry-Rot Facts

The Fungi Only Ever Destroys Timber

While these rots may take nutrients from brick, mortar and plaster, they cannot damage these materials, but can live in them for considerable periods, requiring radical sterilization methods. Structural timber replacement is relatively straightforward, and you rarely need to remove brickwork or masonry (unless to gain access to a cavity), although plaster removal and replacement is always necessary if strands have penetrated walls.

Floorboard removed to show massive dry rot outbreak in the underfloor area.

A rotten splintered timber, completely ravaged by dry rot.

Mushroom-like growths of dry rot on the underside of a floorboard.

Dry Rot Is Not a Rare Fungus

The spores are everywhere, they just happen to germinate in some places where conditions are appropriate. However, spores are present in extremely high concentrations in infected materials, and can therefore be easily spread to infect other areas; spores can be carried via clothes or footwear.

You Must Employ a Specialist Company, Not a General Builder

Powerful, dangerous and accessible-to-the-trade-only chemicals need to be used correctly and safely, and you'll need an insurance-backed guarantee for any future house sale. There are constant advances and new treatments and techniques, and reputable companies 'in the trade' will be up to speed on all the latest ideas. The Property Care Association (see Chapter 5) is the trade federation to approach for their fully trained members to help you; contact them for a list of people in your area.

It is Impractical to Do the Work Yourself, Even if You are a Proficient DIYer

This is because you need specialist training for the technical aspects, and for the above reasons. However, to cut your costs, a person with building skills can certainly do building/excavation, reinstatement work, and a firm may agree to work with you in this way, but they'll only issue their company guarantee if your work meets their standards.

Get Several Estimates for Remedial Works Treatment Before Deciding

Resist the dry-rot 'fear factor' of elaborate horror stories told by companies wanting to do what strikes you as unnecessary work. It's a fact that the fear of dry rot has resulted in many cases of more damage being caused by the treatment than by the rot itself – indeed, some stately homes have been needlessly demolished. If several reputable, ideally old-established, companies agree on a course of action, they are likely to be telling you the truth. Always disbelieve someone attempting to exaggerate the problem in order to scare you.

Remedial Work Can Be Fairly Destructive

It normally involves the removal of plasters and drilling into brickwork to inject chemicals, as well as wholesale replacement of affected timbers.

Fungus-Ridden Timber and Adjacent Areas Must Be Handled Carefully

Protective measures must be taken when handling infected materials: gloves, mask and overalls have to be worn, and contaminated matter must not contact any other areas. The spores should not be inhaled, as they may be harmful to health. Spores can be spread to other places on your shoes and clothes.

Dry Rot is Easier to Control In Eighteenth and Nineteenth-Century Buildings

Old 'soft' wood – almost a contradiction in terms – is much harder than today's softwood timber, and consequently more inherently resistant to attack.

If Your Home is Grade I or Grade II* Listed, You Need to Contact Your Local Conservation Officer Before Starting

This is because you are likely to need Listed Building Consent for certain jobs. In some circumstances, English Heritage may consider giving a grant.

Standard Insurance Policies Do Not Provide Cover Against Fungal Attack

Rots are regarded as an avoidable problem because they are caused by dampness, which is a consequence of neglect or bad maintenance.

Typical wet rot decay in a timber.
Property Care Association

Wet rot and decay in a rotten window frame and sill.

History of Wood Rots

It is assumed that dry rot reached Britain in infected timbers imported from Europe during the fifteenth century; some sources consider it to be indigenous to the Himalayas. The fungus attacked softwood on ships, and occasionally cargos of timber from America and Europe were completely destroyed in this way before they even reached port. In 1810, the newly launched ship *Queen Charlotte* was found to be heavily infected with 'the dry rot', leading to an investigation by the Navy Office, which in 1815 produced its conclusions and published *A Treatise on the Dry-Rot*. Prior to the arrival of dry rot, timber decay agents of this kind were collectively called common or wet rot, with 'the dry rot' being a new phenomenon.

The early investigations sometimes misdiagnosed 'brown rot' (which is actually of the wet variety) as dry rot, and christened common (or 'wet') rot, as 'white rot'. German botanist Robert Hartig established in 1878 that the fungus actually caused the damage, instead of just living on the timber as a secondary problem. Up until the first half of the twentieth century, various fungi, now considered as wet rots, were described as dry rot, but eventually it was agreed that only *Serpula lacrymans* should be referred to as such, and was accordingly termed 'true dry rot'. The conclusion of Forest Products Research Lab in 1963 was that the crucial difference between *Serpula lacrymans* and all the others

Paint and filler conceal wood rot, which has caused the withered appearance of this windowsill.

Rotten window frames and sill partially removed.

was that spores of the former can grow through walls and over inert surfaces, whereas wet rots remained localized. In fact some species of wet rot will grow over or through walls, but this is not normally the case.

Until around 1750, most structural timbers were hardwoods, which were susceptible to white rot damage, characterized by apparent rotting from the outside surface in; this decay was thought to be caused by wind and rain, hence its name: wet rot. However, after the middle of the eighteenth century, softwoods were imported and gradually replaced indigenous hardwoods; these Baltic softwoods, once they were damp, acquired 'brown rot', which left the timber apparently untouched with a sound outer skin, yet was ravaged inside. This concealed decay was caused, they thought, by 'internal fermentations' not water, and was called dry rot, to differentiate it from the weather-caused wet rot. In consequence, earlier dry rots referred to many other brown rots, not as is now the case, *Serpula lacrymans* alone. In 1784 it was accepted that all rots required water: it was once thought that dry rot could 'make' its own water to attack timber, not needing an external moisture source.

What to Look For

Wet rot is apparent as either brown rots that darken wood and cause cuboid cracks (along and across grain) and make it soft and spongy, or white rots, which bleach the wood and make it fibrous. If there are fungus strands, these are usually yellow or black.

Dry rot features either free-standing mushroom shapes of fungus, or spongy growths lying along the timber: the latter are fluffy white or pearly grey mycelium with lilac and canary yellow tinges, grey or white strands and strangely shaped fruiting bodies. One type of outbreak looks like a mass of whitish cobwebby foam. Red dust – spores – can easily be accidentally transported to other parts of the building. Characteristic features can also be grey strands, white growths or grey sheets with yellow-and-violet markings. The rotted wood is lightweight, dark coloured, with cube-like cracks and crumbles at a touch. Sometimes there's a characteristic smell, redolent of rotting tree stumps in a forest.

Causes

Dampness and stagnant air, caused by building faults allowing water to enter the timber and

Rot fungus growing through paint in a door which is only two years old but has been subjected to continuous damp.

RIGHT: **Dry rot fruits on a hall table.**
Ridout Associates

BELOW: **Rotten floor joists, the decayed ends set into a stone wall.**
Property Care Association

(usually) insufficient ventilation. Wet rots thrive when the timber's moisture content is above 35 per cent, whereas dry rot requires a level of 20–35 per cent (*see* Chapter 6 for details of the types and causes of damp). It was once common practice to set timber floor-joists directly into brickwork, and these brick-enclosed timber ends often absorbed dampness from the masonry, which is a common cause of wood rot and structural collapse. When reinstating this kind of floor, it is best to separate the joist timber from the wall itself, ideally by hanging it on a steel joist hanger (*see* Glossary).

Cures – What a Company is Typically Likely to Do

Basically, wet rots simply need to have the damp ingress (and ventilation problem, if any) solved, the

rotten timber replaced with preservative-treated new wood and the area coated with anti-fungicidal chemicals. Dry rot requires this and more besides.

In the past, drastic anti-dry rot chemical treatment was advocated that today would be considered as overkill and unnecessarily harmful to the environment. Similarly, a blowlamp flame used to be trained on the plaster-less brickwork to kill the spores, whereas now this is considered to be unnecessary. Indeed, since removal of water and the introduction of ventilation will kill the fungus, some experts advocate no chemical treatments at all, simply allowing the outbreak to stop by removing these factors. For an inhabited building, however, this is considered to be impractical

Rotten skirting boards: the rippling behind the paint is typical of wet rots. Property Care Association

Burgeoning mushrooms of dry rot. Property Care Association

by many, since it means leaving the damaged area, e.g. an under-floor space, opened up for a long period. The usual compromise is to use some carefully considered chemical treatments, coupled with the building repair measures. There is controversy about the use of chemicals, which can adversely affect the environment, but it's fair to say that it can be practical to treat some timbers in this way as a temporary stopgap.

Expert Quote

Brian Ridout, of Ridout Associates:

Buildings take a long time to dry down – sometimes years. Chemicals can stabilize the timber during this critical period.

Rotten timber joists set in a damp wall. Property Care Association

Close-up of rotten timber. Property Care Association

Tackling Wet Rot

1. Open up the area (e.g. loft space, under-floor cavity or under stairs), raising boards or removing materials, as necessary, to establish the extent of the problem.
2. Ascertain where the dampness is coming from: for instance, for a ground floor ensure the damp-proof course (DPC) is not broken or bridged by raised earth levels outside. Make sure moisture is not coming in from an external source, e.g. a leaking pipe or penetrating damp through the wall. Cure these faults.
3. Introduce ventilation. Make sure air-bricks are not blocked, and, if there are no apparent sources of ventilation, introduce these via new air-bricks.
4. Remove damaged timber and replace it.

Tackling Dry Rot

1. Wearing gloves, mask and overalls, open up the area without tampering with the infected timber. Take care not to walk across the infected timbers without changing shoes before going anywhere else.
2. Spray the rot to 'stabilize' it and let this dry before handling the material too much, in order to reduce the danger of spreading.

3. Remove the infected materials, to 460mm (18in) beyond the outbreak.
4. Remove plaster from nearby walls, in case the fungus has spread to these areas.
5. Drill holes in the brickwork (or stonework) and inject high-performance anti-dry rot chemicals (ideally a paste).
6. Paint all bare brickwork (or stonework) and exposed timber with anti-dry rot chemical-type preparation.

Layer of brown dry rot spores covering the surface of a Jacuzzi. Ridout Associates

7. Eliminate incoming moisture and introduce more ventilation (stages 2 and 3 in 'Tackling Wet Rot' above).
8. Replace timber with double-vacuum preservative-treated material.
9. Replace plaster with special cement-sand rendering mix.
10. Reinstate final finishes and redecorate.

Case Study

The paste, chemical and gun used for injecting the chemical paste into brickwork.

Subject:
Victorian terrace house, mid-row, 280mm (11in) cavity brick wall construction, with a double-slate DPC. Discovered by viewing large area of white fungus underneath floor when a board was raised. This clung to timber surfaces, and around wires and pipes. The house was known to have had a previous outbreak of dry rot, which had been treated several years ago, ineffectively.

Done by:
Warren Woodworm and Waverly Building Preservation Ltd, in association with householder (myself) who did the non-professional general building/ joinery work only, which was masterminded, supervised and inspected by the company.

Diagnosis:
Floorboard integrity was bad beside the front door. On raising a board, an area around 1.2m (4ft) from the front door and spreading backwards into the room, was covered in a white/grey foamy fungus, completely covering wires, pipes and timber.

Dry-rot killer fluid and pump, used to kill the active fungus under the floor before removing the detritus, used by dry rot eradication company.

Reasons for the Outbreak

1. Externally the front doorstep and ground levels to the floor of reception room were higher than the DPC, therefore meaning the moisture was transferred through the wall to the timber.
2. Lack of underfloor ventilation (one small air-brick only at the front, nothing at the back).
3. Additionally, a concrete-floored extension had been built against the back of the property, blocking ventilation at the back of the under-floor area.
4. On raising the boards, the sub-floor was earth and found to be barely an inch below the floor joists, with much evidence of snail trails, therefore indicating that moisture levels were too high and water was soaking into the timber, and was unable to evaporate naturally.

Treatment

Excavation/chemical application:

1. Removal of plaster on the side and front walls adjacent to the outbreak, to a height of 122cm (4ft). All floorboards were raised, discarding any affected by rot.

Removing plaster from the wall using bolster and club hammer.

Massive dry rot outbreak. It has devoured several floor joists and the fungus is covering water and electricity service pipes.

Spraying dry-rot killer fluid under the floor area.

2. Surface sterilization of the main areas of fungus itself. This effectively 'kills' the spores, making their handling and removal less harmful to health.
3. Removal of all affected timber, taking 610–920mm (2–3ft) beyond the visibly affected part.
4. Excavation and removal of earth below the floor, to give at least 150mm (6in) of air-space below the underside of the new floor joists.
5. Laying of 50–75mm (2–3in) of concrete onto the soil surface to seal it and stop snails, worms and insects gaining access to the underfloor cavity.
6. Excavation of earth outside at the front abutting the property, so that the external soil level was 150mm (6in) below the slate DPC.
7. Chemical anti-dry rot paint treatment applied to the underfloor masonry surfaces, and to all exposed healthy timber.
8. Holes drilled in exposed brick walls at specified intervals, and chemical preservative paste injected.

The brickwork here below floor level and just above it has been painted with white anti-dry rot paint to protect against further outbreaks.

Drilling holes in the wall.

Pumping fluid into the holes so as to saturate the wall.

Excess fluid runs down the wall's surface.

TOP LEFT: **Beginning to cut a hole in exterior brickwork in order to fit the large metal air-brick.**

BELOW LEFT: **New concrete step fitted to replace the rotten old timber one.**

9. Three 175 × 150mm (9 × 6in) metal air-bricks fitted into the front wall, below DPC level, to permit air-ventilation. These were covered at the top to seal off the cavity, so that air-flow would be directed beneath the floor. Two air-bricks were inserted into the wall at the rear of the property to allow a front-to-back flow of air.

10. The integrity of the DPC was checked and found to be functioning correctly.

Renewal

1. Concrete doorstep installed, to replace rotted timber one.

2. Bricks taken out of the front wall inside, to allow access to the cavity to make sure it was clear of rubble and debris, which could breach the space and allow dampness to penetrate.

Inside the house, showing plaster and bricks removed from the wall beside the front door.

3. New timber floor joists (double-vacuum preservative treated) installed. The ends of these new joists were kept clear of outside walls, and separated from supportive masonry by a damp-proofing material. All saw-cuts were treated with preservative.

4. New preservative-treated floorboards were installed.

ABOVE: **The new preservative-treated floor joists in position.**

RIGHT: **New preservative-treated floorboards fitted.**

Woodworm damage to end of joint. Property Care Association

5. Bare brick walls were painted with anti-dry rot paint.
6. Walls were re-plastered using special sand/cement render coat with water retardant additives (supplied by the damp-proofing company).
7. New skirting boards were fitted after being double-vacuum preservative treated and these were isolated from brickwork with a damp-proofing membrane.

Expert Quote

Julian Owen, of Julian Owen Associates:

Dry rot can actually spread all around a property and it may not be visible until you start taking the timbers off. You may expect a surveyor to check for something like that but sometimes they cannot access under-floor areas. You can normally smell dry rot to a certain extent, for instance in a cellar. Remember, if it's down underneath the floorboards where you can't get at it, it still spreads through the house.'

WOOD-BORING INSECT INFESTATIONS

Just as with rot, insects attack damp, unventilated timber, and the most common type is woodworm, otherwise known as common furniture beetle. Less common wood-eaters are wood weevils and house longhorn beetles, not forgetting the hard-to-kill deathwatch beetle, which only attacks hardwood. The holes that indicate attack are called 'flight holes', and are made by the insects as they emerge from the timber they've been eating. Generally, insects thrive in warm, moist conditions: central heating reduces relative humidity, thus deterring beetle attack. Treatment is to reduce the moisture content of timber and to use a method to kill the insects, normally some form of insecticide. The problem is getting the poison to reach the insect larvae within the wood, for which reason insecticides are sometimes pumped into the flight holes under pressure.

Wood-Boring Insect Facts
Woodworm Can Either be 'Active' or Dead.
The presence of holes in timber is very often indicative of a long-dead infestation that you can ignore providing the timber's strength is not

compromised. A live infestation is usually indicated by holes and fine wood dust, termed 'frass', this dust becoming more apparent when you tap the timber.

It Is Reasonably Straightforward to Treat. You can treat a minor outbreak yourself, by replacing the affected timber and applying wood-

worm fluid, coupled with addressing any cause of dampness. A major outbreak needs professional treatment, including wholesale chemical spraying, called 'fogging'.

Woodworm Infestations Can Spread Quickly. Woodworm-infected furniture can spread to floorboards and skirtings, even if

Woodworm damage along the edge of joist.
Property Care Association

Woodworm damage to timber.
Property Care Association

they're not damp. Always remove infected furniture or timber as a priority.

Beetles Affect Only the Timber, Never Masonry. Unlike rots, masonry and plaster is unaffected, so invasive demolition is unnecessary.

Employ a Firm That Offers a Thirty-Year Guarantee. You'll need this for a future house sale. The trade body is the PCA, who have members countrywide (*see* Chapter 5).

The Type of Pest Can be Confirmed by Analysing the Frass (the fine wood dust that is the waste product created by insect infestation). A specialist is likely to know by looking, but any doubts can be confirmed by tests.

It's Vital to Identify the Species and the Extent of the Infestation Correctly. Then you can draw up a plan of action. A reputable company will tell you precisely where problems exist and which timbers are unaffected, then explain exactly what's to be done and offer a guarantee. Don't be panicked into rash decisions and beware of specialists who want to swamp everything with chemicals: this is rarely necessary.

Wood Borers Attack New Wood. It is a popular fallacy that woodworm only attacks old houses – new timber is equally at risk. No house, even one recently built, is safe from timber decay.

Cure

The best type of insecticide penetrates deep into wood, ideally through flight holes, and has a residual effect on larvae, pupa and the emerging adult beetles. So the chemical on the timber's surface merely kills eggs, young larvae that hatch on the wood's surface plus the emerging adults. Therefore, the aim of the insecticide is twofold: to prevent further damage done by the larvae inside the timber and to provide a residual poisonous effect on the timber's surface, so as to protect against any possible future attack.

For a minor outbreak you can just paint the timber with woodworm fluid and inject it into any holes, cure any cause of dampness, increase ventilation, if necessary, and renew any badly affected timbers. For a bigger outbreak, a specialist company will renew timbers, repair building faults and spray chemical killers at high concentrations.

Lifecycle of a Wood Borer

All species have a similar pattern of growth and behaviour. This begins with between twenty and forty tiny eggs being laid by the adult beetle on any suitable rough surface, typically a crack or flight hole or timber's end grain. The grub hatches into a larva and starts boring into wood as it feeds on the material's cellulose, a process that can continue for several years, creating a network of tunnels that may interconnect beneath the timber's surface. When the larva is mature it forms a pupa or chrysalis and emerges from the wood as an adult through a flight hole. The adults then mate, lay eggs and die within a few weeks. Larvae can be present deep inside the wood, meaning that timber insecticide applied to the timber's surface cannot always reach them. The lifecycle varies considerably, with woodworm being 3–5 years, and deathwatch beetle being 1–12 years.

Insecticides

These liquids are normally now water-based emulsions, and are applied by brush or spray, contrasting with previous oil-based products, now considered harmful to the environment. Pastes or 'bodied emulsion', aka 'mayonnaise' are contact insecticides in a jelly-like emulsion paste with a high oil solvent content; they stick to timber surfaces and deliver a large quantity of the ingredient. Smoke treatments can be released in a building or a void such as a ceiling space, and leave a fine deposit on the insides of all surfaces the smoke reaches, which kills beetles, eggs and hatching larvae, but not the larvae inside the wood.

Beetle Facts

Common Furniture Beetle
(Woodworm, *Anobium punctatum*)

Small brown beetle, about 3mm (⅛in) long, indicated by the presence of flight holes, about 1mm (1/16in) diameter. Accounts for 75 per cent of all woodworm damage in the UK. It cannot thrive below 12 per cent moisture content in timber.

Wood-Boring Weevils
(*Euophyrum confine* and *Pentarthrum huttoni*)

These require damp timber and fungi, and can normally be killed by drying out the timber. Size: 3–5 mm (⅛–¼in); colour: blackish brown; with 1mm (¹⁄₁₆in) diameter flight-holes. This is the second most widespread wood pest.

House Longhorn
(Camberley beetle, *Hylotrupes bajulus*)

The largest of the wood borers at 13mm (½in) long, leaving an oval flight-hole about 9 × 4mm (⅜ × ³⁄₁₆in). Prevalent only in pre-1950 buildings in North Surrey, and confined to this English county. Their tunnels usually crisscross to form a powder-like mass beneath a thin, intact, external veneer of timber, which may develop corrugations; this is caused by larvae burrowing just beneath.

Deathwatch Beetle (DWB)
(Xestobium rufovillosum)

Attacks old hardwoods, typically in old churches. About 6mm (¼in) long, with round flight-holes 3mm (⅛in) in diameter. Common in southern England, less so in the north and unknown in Scotland. The attack only ever begins in damp timber, but once the creature is within the wood, it can continue to thrive in relatively dry conditions. Extremely hard to eradicate. One approach is to drill holes and inject bodied emulsion paste into the timber. The majority of DWB attacks in historic buildings died out many years ago, often centuries before. The number of flight holes does not necessarily represent the extent of damage done. Insecticide applied to the outside of timber is of little use, and the hardness of the timber (typically dense oak) makes drilling access holes difficult, especially as the larvae are very deeply buried. It's frequently a chronic problem in old buildings, which can be impossible to combat; you just have to treat it periodically and live with it.

Powder Post Beetle
Not a common pest. It only attacks the sap of hardwoods.

RATS AND MICE

The national organization for pest controllers, who

History of the Deathwatch Beetle

This pest got its name from being heard traditionally during the 'death watch' when relatives of a newly deceased person would wait in church to watch over the corpse, to guard against body snatchers. In the silence they would hear the characteristic tapping – the male rapping its head against timber in a mating ritual – high up in the rafters. This grim association presumably encouraged the superstition that a new 'tapping' presaged a death. The deathwatch beetle's natural predator is the house spider, and an unwelcome side-effect of using insecticides to kill these beetles means that their predators are also killed.

In 1668, Mr Wilkins, an Englishman, studied the lifecycle of this pest, then de Geer, in 1774, first described the beast, giving it the name *Xestobium rufovillosum*. Many medieval buildings today, notably old churches in Holland and London (e.g. Westminster Hall, built 1394–99) have been fighting deathwatch beetle infestations continually, succeeding merely in controlling the numbers rather than eradicating them completely.

---

have lists of members in your area, is the British Pest Control Association (BPCA) (www.bpca.org.uk; 01332 294288). This is a not-for-profit organization that represents the interests and development of its members and acts for the pest-management industry within the UK, with a 'Find a member' service on their website.

Facts About Rodents

Chew and Destroy a Building's Fabric. The teeth of these creatures are harder than mild steel, and constantly growing, meaning they have to chew all the time to wear them down. They'll bite through plaster, electrical cables (causing fire dangers), metal pipes, timber and plastic.

Spread Diseases Through Their Urine. Weil's disease, typhus and salmonella are included in the illnesses they can spread when they walk across food (mice have leaking, weak bladders).

Mice Eat Mostly Seeds and Grains. However, they love soap and potatoes, chocolate and even peanut butter, and nowadays are not keen on cheese.

Rats Usually Live in Streams and Sewers. They rarely live in your house – they forage to and from your home for food.

Mice Nest in your Home. Under floorboards, in your shed, loft spaces or anywhere dark and ideally with a handy food source. A popular mouse locale is in a little-used low-level cupboard with stored foods to eat.

A 'Hunter' Cat May Bring a Dead Mouse or Rat in From Outside. So don't necessarily assume you're infested on this evidence alone.

Pest Controllers Cannot Guarantee Their Work. Because they cannot know if a householder is going to take precautions against their return.

Professional Pest Controllers Have Access to Rodent Baits that are Unavailable to the Public. The baits that are generally available will not have the same efficacy as those used by the trade.

They are Mostly Nocturnal Creatures. Making them hard to find in daylight.

Rats

Nowadays rats are an increasing problem, and if they enter your house, they can not only chew through timber, plaster, metal pipes and electrical cables, but can also spread diseases via their droppings and urine (amongst these is deadly Weil's disease). Their average size is about that of a kitten, but the long tail gives illusion they're bigger. The brown rat, *Rattus norvegicus*, is the most usual, the black rat being much rarer. The presence of rats does not necessarily indicate dirt and squalor, since they travel to and from their lair. Rats normally live near streams or in sewers, needing a source of water, so recent cracks or faults in underground drains, in your own house or nearby, can explain rat presence, as can other kinds of building work that interferes with the drainage system in some way. Alternatively, they may have been attracted by a nearby rubbish source – perhaps a nearby café's waste bins.

Generally, they live in either the sewers or in earth burrows near a house, but they have established habits of trekking out to your house to forage for food, then back again, and they always need a water source. Increasingly they are found to be living underneath timber decking in back gardens. The usual approach to getting rid of them is to call in a professional, who lays anticoagulant poisonous bait.

Even if you just suspect rats are in the vicinity, it makes sense to examine every possible place of entry – quite small holes allow this – and block it up to proof them out; under-floor foundations sometimes have access holes, and if there's simply earth below your floor this is a potential entry point. But never block air-bricks, which must always remain clear – their holes are too small to allow entry of rodents.

Mice

These attractive little creatures have a slender pointed nose, a hairless tail and are greyish brown with a grey or buff belly. They like to eat seeds and grain, and are inquisitive and eager to investigate new surroundings. Mice have weak bladders and constantly leak urine onto food, which can spread the same diseases as those carried by rats. Likely sites to find them in your home are rarely-opened cupboards, sheds or under the floorboards. They are attracted by warmth and food; rice, soap, potatoes and even candles can be their typical fare, with which they like to live, if possible. Mice can 'collapse' their bodies in order to get through very small holes into your home. They do not need a water supply and are nocturnal. A mouse nest is likely to be 100–150mm (4–6in) in diameter, and made of paper or something similar. Not reliant on a water source, as rats are, they get sufficient moisture from their food. Litters of five to six young are born nineteen to twenty-one days after mating, and the rodents are sexually mature at 6–10 weeks. In addition to chewing building fabric they are known for eating documents, books, paintings and so on.

Getting Rid of Rodents

The usual extermination method is by baiting with anticoagulant poisons. The strongest of these is unavailable to the public, and a professional pest exterminator knows the best situations in which to use them. Rats, who don't usually live in the house, go away to die – often in search of water, since a strong thirst is a side-effect of the poison. With luck, mice may also do so, but unfortunately may also die

What to Look For

Rats
- Sultana-sized dark droppings – a rat gives 40–50 droppings per day.
- Hearing scratching sounds at night.
- Acrid odour, shredded paper denoting a burrow.
- Grey-black grease smears on interior surfaces.
- Footprints in mud, dust or flour or damage to food packets.

Mice
- Small droppings, dark coloured, the size of rice grains – a mouse leaves 40–100 droppings daily.
- Damage to food packets, such as packets of rice with the corners chewed off, especially in low-level cupboards.
- Scuffling noises, mainly at night.

somewhere in your house in an inaccessible place, and if you don't want to lift many floorboards, the only alternative is to wait for the mouse corpse to degrade, and put up with the smell. In many areas, mice are now resistant to the original anticoagulant, warfarin, and alternatives are used instead.

Traps – known in the trade as break-back traps – are also an effective answer. For mice, don't bait these with cheese, but load them with fruit-and-nut chocolate or peanut butter. Place traps close to, and at right angles to, walls, near to where you find droppings or other evidence of activity. Do not buy the cheap plastic traps from supermarkets: their springs are too weak to be effective, they are very hard to set and are likely to injure the poor mouse rather than kill it outright. To inflict a quick, efficient death, opt for the old-fashioned wood-and-powerful-spring type that does the job quickly

and effectively. A test is, when you pull back the bar to set the trap, it should be a noticeably forceful spring, not a weak insipid one that could snap on your finger and not even hurt. For rats, bait the larger traps with part-cooked bacon, placing the devices near their food source.

An alternative is the humane trap, a glass box that automatically closes after the mouse's entrance, allowing you to release the mice unharmed – but always take them a very long way from your house, otherwise they will simply return; it is vital to check humane traps frequently.

One advantage of having a professional is that they have access to more potent poisons, but more importantly, trained operators know how and where to lay baits to gain control quickly. Also, a professional will know how to handle such issues as the question of the threat posed to pets by baits.

Precautions to Deter Rats and Mice

- Clean up spilled rubbish and refuse areas, sweep up food spills, keep pet food in sealed containers, put refuse in lidded dustbins.
- Outdoors, remove rubbish and piles of old vegetation, piles of scrap wood, gathered leaves, weeds and clutter near buildings. Beneath outdoor decking can be an ideal home for rats, so bear this in mind.
- Fix and replace cracked or broken doors and windows. Keep drains and drain covers in a secure state – mice and rats can squeeze through surprisingly small spaces.
- Cover roof-ventilation holes with wire-netting or mesh, so as to proof-out rodents, while not losing the vital ventilation to the roof space.

CHAPTER 9

Materials and How They Are Used

MORTARS, RENDERS AND CONCRETE

Mortars and renders are made from aggregate, meaning sand, mixed with a binder, which is cement or (for very old buildings) non-hydraulic lime. Water is added to the mixture, which activates the binder to work as a glue, bonding the sand particles together, so that when the mixture cures it forms a hard substance, whose additional advantage is that when wet, the mortar or render sticks to bricks and stone, allowing you to build up a solid wall. Concrete is made by mixing sand, pebbles and cement and adding water.

When you're repairing renders or redoing repointing, it is vital to match the material used in the rest of the building, otherwise cracking of the substance and subsequent damp problems will result (see Chapter 6). Generally speaking, only buildings constructed prior to around 1850 are likely to have lime mortar used in their build, as after this date practically all building work was done using cement-based mortars and renders.

How Does the Binder Change and Set Hard?

Cement, when water is added, undergoes a series of chemical reactions that cause its different constituents to crystallize and these crystals to interlock, giving the material strength, which increases steadily during the setting time, up to twenty-four hours if you added no aggregate to cement, it would itself dry to form a rock-like substance. Lime (see below for types of lime) hardens in a completely different way, as a result of a reaction with atmospheric carbon dioxide – termed 'carbonation'; lime mortars and renders harden over a much longer time than cement-based materials, and must not be allowed to dry out too quickly, because a rapidly dried lime mortar or render will result in a low-strength poor-quality building component. Generally, working with lime mortars and renders requires much more skill and knowledge than working with cement-based materials. And, once cured, lime mortars and renders tend to absorb water, as opposed to cement-based materials, which repel water to some extent.

Sands

Essentially, sand consists of fragments of rocks crushed by nature; these are of varying colours according to regions. The most usual sand you get from builders' merchants is yellow coloured. 'sharp' sand – aka 'washed' or 'Thames-washed' sand, feels spiky and prickly when you crush it in your hand, and this is because it has had many of the impurities washed from it, leaving only the pure material. 'Soft' sand – aka 'Building' sand – feels gentle on the hand because it still possesses natural loam and soil particles.

Sharp sand is used for floor screeds, in concrete and for wall renderings. Soft sand is used to make mortar for bricklaying or repointing; its soft, pliable nature is suited to the flexibility of spreading and shaping.

Hydraulic Lime

The source of this material is limestone, which naturally contains a proportion of clay, plus calcium and magnesium carbonates. It is mined mainly in France, and is imported for specialist lime centres, such as Anglia Lime (see Contacts). Certain lime products are available in the form of finely ground powders in different colours: pale buff, light grey or white. When making mortar or render with this you need to afterwards add the minimum amount of water, after which you cannot add any more, to keep it usable. When mixed with aggregates it's referred to as 'coarse stuff' and must be used within four hours. Lime putty is also available.

Portland Cement (Ordinary Portland Cement or OPC)

Made by the mechanical combination of limestone and clay, cement is usually a fine grey powder. The first cement to be patented in England was made by Joseph Aspdin in Leeds in the early 1800s. Hard limestone was crushed and calcined, mixed with clay, then the mix was ground into a fine slurry with water. This mixture was fired, broken into lumps and fired again. In 1838 William Aspdin (Joseph's son) improved the process, then Isaac Johnson improved upon this, so that by the 1850s, cements were similar to those of today. White Portland cement is a slightly weaker variety, that's useful when making mortars, as well as reconstituted, or artificial, stone, which is a kind of 'concrete', made from a mixture of cement, stone powder, sand and water cast in moulds. White cement's advantage is that it does not change the aggregate's natural hue, which grey cement does.

Concrete

A mixture of cement, pebbles and sand that sets hard, and is used extensively in virtually all buildings to create a hard, stone-like material, either underground as a base to build from, or to create a solid floor, amongst other things. When cast in large areas, it is usual to leave expansion gaps that are filled with mastic material, to allow for movement. A standard concrete mix comprises by volume: 1 part cement, 2 parts sand and 4 parts small (10mm or 20mm diameter) pebbles (called pea shingle or gravel). In practice you normally buy the sand and pebbles ready-mixed in the correct ratio, termed 'ballast', in which case the mix is 1 part cement to 6 parts ballast. For a stronger or weaker concrete, the proportion of cement can be adjusted accordingly. To make a small quantity the materials are mixed dry with a shovel, on a hard surface, then water is added slowly, mixing all the time until the correct consistency is achieved. Too wet, and the

mixture may dry weaker than otherwise; too dry and it won't pack into the cavity easily, and may not set properly. Sometimes, for particular situations, concrete with minimal water is specified (termed 'dry packing') because, if this mixture is exposed to the atmosphere, water will always eventually permeate through enough to initiate the setting process; instances might be to pack out a cavity in masonry below a roof joist, so that the resultant concrete is less likely to crack afterwards and offers good structural support.

Large amounts of concrete can be delivered via a mixer lorry, when the material is funelled to its destination using a long, semicircular chute. A concrete mixer is like the concrete lorry in miniature, except to deliver the concrete you have to physically tip up the machine, allowing the turning motion of the drum to direct and drive the wet mixture to its home. The best way to mix concrete in a mixer is to put the requisite water in first, turn on the machine, then add cement, then the ballast.

Renders

Daub (mud/cow dung, straw and water) was originally used, after which lime plasters were used. Basically, lime plaster is a similar material to daub, with lime putty replacing the mud. Exterior decorative renders of this kind were called pargetting. 'Stucco' is the term for gypsum plaster, sand and lime, used for external decoration; it can be shaped and scored so as to look like stone blocks – known as 'false ashlaring' – for instance, to disguise inferior brickwork. Stucco could be enhanced by adding crushed marble, stone dust or fired clay to the mix. Coade stone, invented by Mrs Eleanor Coade in 1760 and made to a secret formula, has a glossy pottery-like finish and was used for ornamentation and embellishment on building exteriors.

Modern renders are either made from sand/cement mixes (or sand/lime mixes for lime-mortared buildings) and applied in three coats: the first one called the 'scratch' coat, scored in criss-cross lines to achieve maximum adhesion for subsequent coats. The key problem with renders are: water penetration – often when dissimilar materials are used; or too strong a mix, when fine cracks can appear after a time, which suck in moisture; when dampness cannot escape it causes decay and degradation.

Different Applied Wall-Finish Render Materials

Stucco: smooth hard material made from lime, sand and water. More modern stuccos may have cement as binder.

Rustication: grooved or channelled joints cut into stucco's surface to simulate expensive ashlar stone block work.

Roughcast/harling: rough-textured traditional render finish, created by mixing gravel with the final coat, which is thrown on.

Pebbledash: pebbles of uniform size are flicked onto a wet render surface, leaving half of the stones protruding, to produce a uniform pattern.

Vermiculation: the carving of a stone surface with an irregular mottled pattern of worm-like ridges, which was created by carving render in the same way, or producing patterned panels from moulds.

Stucco mouldings: exterior decorative mouldings and panels imitating carved stonework – examples being architraves surrounding windows and cornices running horizontally around buildings.

Daub: mixture of clay, straw and cow dung.

Spatterdash: coarse type of rendering, created by flicking render onto the wall.

Tyrolean finish: spray-applied wall finish of render and stone chippings.

Mortars

Mortar is used for bonding brick or stone during construction, the idea being that the malleable material takes up any differences in the thickness of bricks, as well as bonding them together. It is also used for repointing, when the material between bricks or stones becomes loose and friable. The mortar must always match the surrounding materials, otherwise problems will occur. If your house mortar feels soft to the touch, it's likely to be lime/sand mix (prior to 1850 construction), whereas if it feels rock hard it will be a cement/sand mix. If in doubt there are mortar-matching services (*see* Anglia Lime in Contacts), for analysing both the proportion of sand and binder, as well as the colour/type of sand. When doing repointing, you rake out the joints to a depth of about an inch, and, once filled, pointing should always be recessed, never standing out or obtruding above the brick or stone.

BRICK AND BLOCKS

Bricks

Before around 1839 bricks were mostly handmade, meaning that a mixture of clay, other materials and water was packed into moulds then fired in a kiln in batches. After this time bricks were machine-made, and were more uniform in colour and appearance. In 1969 the 'metric brick' arrived, which measures 215 × 102 × 65mm (8½ × 4 × 2½in). Prior to this, sizes were only marginally different, except for the much thinner bricks of the 1500s. 'Facing' bricks are designed to present a good appearance; 'commons' are used for general construction where appearance is not an issue; and 'engineering' bricks have a dense body and a guaranteed minimum compressive strength – used where this aspect is important. As for colour, Georgian bricks were mostly browns, greys and yellows, as well as vernacular shades, such as Staffordshire Blues. Yellow was a very popular London brick colour until 1850. Staffordshire and Lancashire bricks were made from soil with a preponderance of iron, and were bright red. Manganese in South Wales, Berkshire and Surrey made their vernacular bricks blacker. Contrastingly, Hampshire and Oxfordshire bricks tend to be whites and greys, because clays from these counties had a high lime content and no iron. Cracks in brick walls can be repaired, but the initial cause (e.g. timber rotting or iron corroding within the wall) has to be corrected. 'Stitching' is a technique where the damaged bricks are removed either side of the crack line and replaced.

Nowadays common bricks are the cheapest, with a 'frog' (a recession on the top surface that acts to enhance the bonding capacity of the mortar), and there are ranges of other types, 'facings' being those of an attractive appearance; some types of engineering bricks incorporate three large holes through their thickness, as a way of allowing mortar to penetrate these and afford a more robust structure.

Bricks are cut with a 'bolster', a large cold chisel. You position the chisel on each face and strike gently, then strike once on one of the split-lines

Concrete masonry units (CMUs) aka concrete/breeze blocks. B&Q

to crack the brick, on the same principle as tile cutting. A professional bricklayer can cut a brick with one blow.

Blocks: Concrete Masonry Units (CMUs)

Once called breeze blocks, these are made from cast concrete, which is a mixture of cement and various kinds of aggregate. For high-density blocks, sand and fine gravel might be used, whereas lower density, consequently lighter, blocks have industrial waste materials, such as ash, used for their aggregate. A third type of block, growing in popularity, is made using aerated concrete, and the resultant blocks have excellent insulating qualities; large, aerated blocks are often used instead of twin-cavity walls, allowing faster builds with as good, or better, insulation than a cavity-wall construction. Trench blocks are extremely robust concrete masonry blocks suitable for use underground for foundations, as they are unaffected by soil and moisture. Sizes of standard CMUs are 440 × 215 × 100mm (17 × 8½ × 3.9in), and for large, aerated blocks,

intended as a complete wall with no cavity, 440 × 215 × 300 (17 × 8½ × 12in), and they come in other thicknesses. Blocks are relatively soft, and you can cut them with a special, large-toothed saw. The larger 'full wall thickness' aerated blocks and trench blocks have interlocking tongues and grooves along their sides, allowing them to lock together with their neighbours. CMUs are produced by companies including Thermalite and Celcon.

STONE

Usually, local stones were used prior to the mid-nineteenth century and the coming of the railways. Basalt and granite are the hardest stones, and are very resistant to weathering. Limestone can be soluble in water at the surface, and so is subject to surface wear due to weather. However, as a rule, limestone mortar is termed 'sacrificial' because it is designed to draw water by capillary action away from the stone. Sandstones resist wear but attract dirt. Cotswold limestones range from almost white to golden browns and pale buffs. Magnesium limestone/dolomite, in creams, greys and browns is found from Nottinghamshire to Darlington and lias limestone in South Yorkshire and Dorset, while Pennine gritstones and York-stone are sandstones, with red sandstone typical of the midlands and the west country.

Cracking, or spalling, can occur, either through iron inside the wall corroding and expanding, or trapped water freezing and doing the same; what is more, settlement of a building can create fractures. Specialists can replace broken areas with a similar type of stone, which is then dressed and carved to match the rest. An alternative method is to use reconstituted stone (stone powder and cement) produced from a mould for a 'plastic repair' – this is most suitable for small areas.

FLINT

(See Chapter 4)

Flint is a pebble-type stone that is either used as it is or 'knapped', where the stone is split to reveal a glossy blackness. Flint stones are raggedly textured and very hard, and sometimes multicoloured. Types are termed: quarry flint, square knapped, field flint and beach pebbles/cobbles, which are round and not knapped.

TIMBER

Contrary to popular opinion, 'softwood', meaning Baltic and Scandinavian pinewood, has been ubiquitous to Britain since the early 1700s. Prior to this time indigenous oak and elm were used but, due to elm's lack of resistance to decay, very little now survives. Oak, however, can still be functioning well after 500 years, and replacement new 'green' oak is available for repairs to old oak buildings.

However, the term softwood is a slight misnomer, in that old softwood is much harder than the new equivalent, and it is also stable, as opposed to new timber that flexes and moves and warps for a considerable time. Since the majority of timber used in houses since the beginning of the seventeenth century has been softwood, it is either painted or has a dark appearance, due to stains and varnishes; sometimes wood was grained, the swirling grain lines made in the dark stain to give the appearance of costly hardwood. This is why it is usually a mistake to strip timber in a house of its

Wide range of timber planks available in B&Q stores. B&Q

surface finish, as the bare timber is normally full of knots, and was always intended to be covered by paint or stains/waxes. Exceptions are handrails and newel posts, which might have been made from expensive hardwood.

Timber is used extensively in most buildings, and always has been, and is one of the most flexible and aesthetically beautiful natural materials there is. Large timber joists are used in flooring and roofing, boards for flooring are relatively thin, and new buildings are even more dependent on this material: modern timber-framed houses are made by erecting a timber structure, then enclosing this with brick and block-work walls. The majority of newly built houses have hardwood timber windows.

Structural timber is graded for strength, and it's usual for architects or engineers to specify a particular grade for a particular job: for instance, C16 is considered suitable for a degree of load bearing. The grade pertains to relative straightness and lack of knots that could compromise its integrity. These timbers are often sold factory-treated with preservative, and then described as 'tanalized'. After outbreaks of dry rot, it's usual to replace timbers with 'pressure-treated' preservative-treated timbers, as a safeguard against further attack.

When buying timber, whether new or second-hand, always buy from a dealer who has stored the timber correctly, meaning undercover – if it is stored outside, the timber can absorb moisture, so that when it is in your heated home it's likely to shrink and crack. The correct moisture range for timber should be around 9–11 per cent.

Sheet Timber

These are manufactured boards, available in 224 × 122cm (8 × 4ft) sizes, occasionally in smaller dimensions.

Close-up to show the veneers of plywood.

Plywood. Several layers of timber veneers are glued together to make a solid sheet, in thicknesses 4, 6, 9, 12, 18mm (⅛, ¼, ⅜, ½, ¾in). External grade plywood is weather resistant to some extent.

Chipboard. This a fairly soft material, made from small fragments of timber bonded together.

Oriented Strawboard. An engineered wood panel with no voids, made from small pieces of timber bonded together.

Chipboard. B&Q

ABOVE: **MDF boards.** B&Q

BELOW: **Different kinds of stair parts available at B&Q stores and other DIY outlets.** B&Q

Blockboard. Blockboard is a sandwich of timber veneers with a solid core of timber strips inside.

MDF. Medium-density fibreboard is brown-coloured, made of high-pressure packed wood materials stuck together, available in thicknesses 4 and 6mm (³⁄₁₆ and ¼in) (hardboard) as well as 9, 12, 18 and 25mm (³⁄₈, ½, ¾ and 1in), and some types are moisture-resistant. The majority of manufactured kitchen cabinets are made from MDF with a surface covering of coloured plastic.

Mouldings

Mouldings are factory-made lengths of timber cut to a specific cross-sectional profile, used mainly for skirting boards, architraves and picture rails. Profiles are described variously as ogee, torus, bullnose, chamfered, lamb's tongue, Scotia and so on. Decorative mouldings are smaller strips, such as dowels and angle beads for filling gaps or for decoration.

Wide variety of wood stains and varnishes. B&Q

Staircases

You can buy complete timber staircases, as well as factory-made handrails, spindles (banisters) and newel posts.

Wood Stains, Waxes and Varnishes

Wood stains/dyes. These are either water-based or solvent-based, and are dyes that can make a wood darker, but cannot lighten it.

Varnishes. Varnishes sit on the surface and seal the timber.

Oil-Based Polyurethane. Available in finishes matt, satin and high gloss, these liquids are sweet smelling, yellow, waterproof and tough, and give a yellowish tinge to blond timber.

Water-Based Acrylic Varnish. A milky-white liquid that dries to a transparent film. Quick drying, odourless and colourless.

Yacht Varnish. High-gloss finish, this is an oil-based varnish similar to polyurethane, but having better qualities of adhesion, durability and protection. The ideal choice for exterior wood-work.

Varnish Stains (Satin and Gloss). Varnish stains colour and varnish in one operation.

Oils. These seep down into the grain, hardening and protecting it. They give a durable, attractive, non-chip finish, and slightly darken the wood's appearance. Danish oil darkens and enhances grain and is fine for garden furniture and pine. Tung oil darkens, seals and waterproofs.

Waxes. These give a beautiful sheen to timber, and successive layers build to a patina. The main types are beeswax, carnauba, coloured waxes and natural wax mix. Traditionally used for old timber floors, wainscoting (wooden wall panelling) and staircases.

French Polishes. All-embracing term for a wide range of shellac-based polishes of different kinds.

Massive range of plasters available at builders' merchants and DIY outlets. B&Q

PLASTERS

Lime Plaster

This is a traditional material, used prior to the 1930s. It was made from a mixture of lime (produced from crushed limestone) and sand mixed with water, and applied in three coats. If you already have lime plaster that needs repairing, the material is still available.

Gypsum Plaster

This is the standard plaster used today. The earliest from was called Plaster of Paris, made by heating gypsum (a naturally occurring mineral) in a kiln to produce a 'hemi hydrate' and water, which is driven off. The setting process is the reverse, whereby you add water to Plaster of Paris and it sets to hard crystalline gypsum. Building plasters are categorized as: 'Bonding', for bonding to brick and block work and timber; 'Undercoat', for filling major cavities; and 'Finish', used in a very thin layer to produce a glass-smooth final finish. 'Multifinish' is a type of plaster that can be used for several different types of application.

Lath-and-Plaster

This was a method of creating wall and ceiling

finishes used in the past, and is basically plaster reinforced by a skeleton of timbers. Inch-wide thin slats of wood (laths) are nailed to a framework of structural timbers, leaving small gaps between them. Plaster is applied, pushed against the surface so that it oozes through the gaps and locks the plaster in place, then other coat(s) are applied on top.

Plasterboard

This is used for making ceilings, and also for establishing a good flat surface onto brickwork, the latter as an alternative to applying wet plaster. Standard size is 224 × 122cm (8 × 4ft), thicknesses 9 and 12mm (⅜ and ½in), and the edges can be square edge or tapered edge. Tapered-edge boards are so designed that they taper on their long edges, so that when two boards are fitted side by side you're left with a shallow depression that is quite easy to fill, so as to produce a perfectly flat finish. When boards are joined in this way, it's usual to place fibreglass tape across to bridge the joint, which acts as a binder for the filling material.

MATERIALS FOR COVERING FLAT ROOFS

(*See also* Chapter 4.)

Metals

Lead is most common, copper was used historically; both of these are laid in flat panels, their edges folded together in a specific way, so as to form a weatherproof seam. Lead sheet edges are joined at wooden loaf-shaped bars, called rolls – these are screwed to the roof at intervals. Copper panels were joined in a similar way. Zinc was also used, but this cannot be dressed into a corner, unlike malleable lead. Asphalt was also used for porches, bay windows and small extensions, and was poured in two layers up to 1in thick. This material is much heavier than other products and should only be used when the roof has been designed to take the weight. This is rarely used for houses, sometimes for flats.

Edge-on view of plasterboards. B&Q

Roofing Felt

Bitumen-impregnated felt is the waterproof layer, and it is usually in roll form, spread out onto the roof, normally in three layers, the felt overlapping at the edges. For timber-boarded roofs, the usual standard practice is to nail down the first layer, and for panel products it is partially bonded, overlapping the edges, then the next two layers (which also overlap at the edges) are bonded to this first layer in one of the below ways:

Pour and Roll. Hot bitumen is poured in front of the felt as it is unrolled, acting as an adhesive, both to the underneath layer and where it overlaps at the sides.

Torching. This is a special type of felt incorporating a layer or melt-able bitumen on its underside. You heat up this layer with a gas torch immediately prior to unrolling, so that the melted bitumen bonds to the felt beneath as it is unrolled: it also bonds at the sides where it overlaps.

Cold-Applied. Where a cold adhesive is spread onto the roof surface, then the felt unrolled into it, to stick down. Overlaps are also sealed in this way.

Self-Adhesive. Where the underside of the material has an adhesive layer covered with release paper, so that when the paper is removed and the felt rolled out, it sticks to the felt beneath; this is unsuitable for uneven surfaces or for use in cold conditions.

ROOF TILES

Battens are nailed horizontally to the roof's main timbers at measured intervals, to which the rows of slates or tiles are fixed. More recent roofs have roofing felt fitted beneath tiles, but older roofs did not, and you should never add felt where there was none previously, because vital ventilation is restricted. Most tiles have 'nibs' – projections at the top end that hook over battens, and can additionally be nailed through pre-cast holes (often tiles are nailed every fourth row). Very old tiles had holes for oak pegs that also hooked over battens. Slates are nailed to the timbers via pre-punched holes. Tiles are usually hung 'double lap', meaning each row half covers the one beneath, as well as overlapping the top part of the row beneath that.

Rows are set so that slate or tile gaps are staggered, each occurring halfway along the width of the one beneath (to allow this, tiles of one-and-a-half size width are used on alternate rows at the verges). 'Single-lap' fixing is where tiles only overlap one row beneath, used for interlocking tiles, such as Roman and French tiles, whose side joints lock together to form a waterproof joint (see *below*).

For a hipped roof, 'bonnet' or 'half round' tiles are used to join the roof planes, and these sit over the gap between the tiled roof panels – these can also be used for slated roofs if the colours match. To bridge the gap between the roof planes of a gabled roof, specially shaped ridge tiles or even iron stanchions are used, these items linking the roof planes by sitting astride the gap and resting against both surfaces. Bonnet and ridge tiles are bedded onto a weak mortar mix.

Flashings, arrangements of lead strips, are used to bridge the gaps between roof coverings and chimneys or walls. Bendable lead is usually formed to shape *in situ*, with its top parts embedded in mortar courses. Mortar fillings (listings), were also used for this purpose but often crack and fail.

Plain Tiles

Rectangular units available in over fifty colours. Single camber tiles have a slight camber along their length, whereas double-camber tiles are also arched from side to side. Shaped tiles are produced in many designs (e.g. club, diamond, bullnose and fishtail) and were sometimes hung in alternate rows to plain tiles to enhance the decorative effect – shaped tiles are a common feature of Victorian roofs.

Profiled Tiles

These give the roof an undulating appearance. Roman tiles are made of 'under tiles' fixed flat and barrel shaped, and half-round 'over tiles'. Spanish tiles are similar to Roman ones, except that they have a concave under tile and a convex over tile. Pantiles are a variation of the Spanish tile and French tiles interlock at the sides, top and bottom, and are not nailed.

Slates

Slates are made from split-able stone, which is dressed to the correct thickness and size. There

Huge range of fillers, all for different applications. B&Q

is either 'natural slate' or the much heavier 'stone slate'. Materials are either sandstone or limestone, or modern man-made slate, made from fibre cement and concrete (originally made from asbestos cement). The surface texture varies from smooth to riven. Colours are greens, blues, greys, purples and reds. Sizes are described as 'smalls', 'doubles', 'ladies', 'countesses' and 'duchesses'. The thinnest are termed 'bests', the thickest 'strongs', with 'mediums' in between. They are fixed in position by nailing using pre-punched holes.

MATERIALS FOR FILLING CAVITIES

These are plasters, normally white, that dry hard and are designed to blend with solid building materials, e.g. plaster and wood, to make repairs that are afterwards covered with paint. Standard fillers are often called decorator's caulk.

They come either as a powder you mix with water, ready mixed in a tub or in a cartridge-type tube, for gun application. They are applied with a filling knife or direct from the cartridge: the nozzle

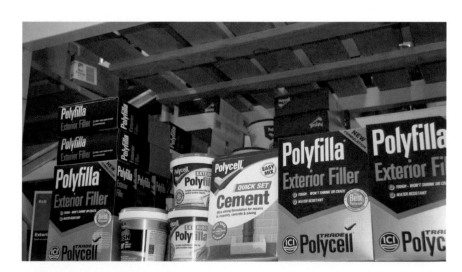

Exterior fillers. B&Q

Interior fillers. B&Q

can be trimmed so as to deliver a neat bead. They can either be smoothed while wet, or applied slightly proud of the surface and sanded down once dry. You should fill to a depth of no more than 9mm (⅜in) at a time, unless you use the special 'deep fill' range. Important aspects of a good filler is its softness and how easy it is to smooth down afterwards (if necessary). The company 'Toupret' make a range of extremely high quality fillers.

A useful tip is to use a gun-applied type filler with a small nozzle hole for filling any cracks around window rebates or internal corners generally, as they can perfectly soften a harsh right angle. You get a perfect rounded fill, finished off by simply running your finger along the surface, so there is no need to sand afterwards.

Flexible Filler

Usually a cartridge application, you load the canister in a 'skeleton'-type application gun. This is ideal wherever there's likely to be shrinkage and movement, notably for filling the cracks between skirting boards and the wall (as above, just fill, then run a finger along the surface).

Fine Surface Filler/Spackle

Ready-mixed paste in a tub. This is an extremely fine filler that can be used for obliterating the tiniest blemishes, e.g. to smooth the depressions of fine wood-grain lines. It can be used effectively to fill wood-grain lines on painted timber (so long as the gloss surface is removed) or on bare timber itself. Use of the supplied plastic spreader allows you to clear the 'peaks', while the troughs are filled. It responds well to superfine sanding with fine-grade sandpaper.

Deep-Gap Filler

Just like an ordinary filler but you can fill to depths deeper than 9mm (⅜in) at a time.

'No More Sanding' (Polyfilla Brand Name)

An unbelievably light filler that is so incredibly fine that it's easy to smooth it to a perfect finish with your filling knife, so that sanding is not required. This filler is made using microscopic glass beads, and is only suitable for interior use.

Hairline-Crack Filler

Usually in a tube dispenser or applied by brush from a tin. Since it dries in a very short time, it's ideal for use immediately prior to decorating, if minor blemishes suddenly become apparent.

Wood Filler

This is a resin-based material for external or internal timber repairs, designed to bond firmly to bare timber. It comes as a wood-coloured paste and a white tube of catalyst, which, when mixed together in the correct proportions, dries rock hard. Fill proud of the surface and sand down afterwards. Often used in combination with 'Wood hardener', which is a resin-based liquid that effectively strengthens and solidifies timber that has been weakened and softened over time: apply this by brush and it penetrates deep into the timber. Remember, you have to make sure the timber has dried out before using these materials. Some manufacturers make it in different colours, and it can be painted afterwards; however, if you're staining or varnishing you'll need to match the colour to your wood. Using wood fillers can be an effective way of repairing damaged timber at a superficial cosmetic level, but if any structural timber is affected, or if too much of any timber area is effected by rot, it's best to replace the timber completely.

Expanding Foam

This is merely for filling large cavities quickly with polystyrene foam, which adheres firmly to almost anything. It has no inherent strength at all but serves to fill gaps, e.g. those left when a pipe goes through a wall or if a doorframe has gaps between itself and the adjacent bricks or blocks. You squirt in the liquid from the aerosol canister, the foam expands inside the hole to many times its size, the bubble-filled material normally oozing from the open side. It can be trimmed back afterwards when cured. Always wear protective gloves, as this material adheres firmly to skin.

SEALANTS

These are always ready mixed and always come in applicator cartridges, either for use in the skeleton gun, or using the dispenser itself. They are either water-based 'acrylic polymers' that can be over-painted or 'silicones', which cannot. They are applied by introducing a bead of sealant in the channel you want filled, which is afterwards smoothed carefully with a finger or the purpose-made smoother. It forms a fragile surface skin within seconds, which later rubberizes completely, meaning that after smoothing for the first time, there are no second chances. Totally flexible, making these products ideal for filling gaps between materials that are prone to movement, such as timbers or plastic bonded to brick. Sealant can never be sanded or shaped afterwards. Never economize and buy

Different kinds of sealants, for different applications. B&Q

cut-price sealants, go for a well-known brand name: inferior sealants can quickly lose their colour, and some may not adhere effectively.

Frame Sealant

Either acrylic or silicone, made in a range of colours, and designed principally for filling the gaps around windows and door frames. Bonds perfectly to plaster, brick, aluminium and UPVC.

Bathroom Sealant
or Sanitary Sealant

This is a silicone, specifically formulated for filling gaps around baths, sinks, basins, shower trays and so on. It sticks so well to porcelain that it's practically impossible to pull it off if you make a mistake. Available in white or translucent.

Gutter and Roof Sealant

Black rubberized sealant for permanent water-resistance and weatherproofing, intended for sealing cavities in gutters, downpipes and flashings, and should be suitable for repairing flat roofs, but this is likely to be a temporary measure only.

ADHESIVES

These work by bonding themselves to the surface of the two materials, via microscopic 'hooks'. Using the correct adhesive is imperative, particularly because some materials, such as wood and cardboard, are porous and require an adhesive that sinks into the surface, while metals and plastics are impervious and the bonding agent clings to the surface alone. Adhesives are either water-based or solvent-based, some are gap-filling, while others need to have perfect mating surfaces to work properly. The same products are made by a number of manufacturers.

Contact Adhesive

Strongly smelling solvent adhesive that is virtually impossible to shift once in place and typically used for joining sheet materials. Spread a thin layer on each surface, allow to dry for a brief period, then position and push together and there is an immediate grip, making it impossible to remove. There is also a variety that allows you to slide the pieces for a moment before final fixing. It is messy to use and

Range of adhesives. B&Q

Epoxy resins, and various other types of adhesive for small-scale applications. B&Q

virtually impossible to remove if it spills. Used for plastics, timber, textiles, plus other materials.

PVA Adhesives

These water-based adhesives are great for porous materials, such as timber or cardboard. It's a white liquid, simple and clean to use, and easy to clean from surfaces. However, it has only a limited initial 'grab' for which reason you need to clamp or screw the materials tightly together until the initial set takes place; exceptions to this are for light pieces of timber fixed to larger timbers, whose initial suction stays permanent, because there are no gravitational forces pulling it apart. Definitely not gap-filling – you need matching surfaces.

Epoxy Resins

'Araldite' is one familiar name that makes epoxy resins, and the brand name is synonymous with the glue. It gives an extremely strong bond and is often the only adhesive that is suitable for materials such as metals, though it can be used for most rigid mater-ials; it is most suited to metals, plastics and wood. A resin and hardener are mixed in equal quantities – the dispenser is often of a 'double barrelled' design so you squeeze out equal amounts automatically. There's a 'rapid' type that dries quicker than the standard epoxy. Professional resin-based adhesives are used by specialist contactors for repairing masonry, since they are amongst the most powerful adhesives known, and some can be mixed with powdered brick or stone to make an effective filler that bonds perfectly.

Super Glue/Cyanoacrylate

This comes in tiny dispensers, because it's usually used for small-scale repairs. It will bond most materials and there's virtually an instant, excellent bond on application. When it's applied the glue thickens and hardens to create a very strong bond.

Don't get it on your skin, because it sticks skin as effectively as anything else, and has been used as dangerous 'handcuffs' by criminals smearing it on people's palms and pressing them together. Definitely not gap-filling – you need good, tight-fitting mating surfaces. The usual type is a clear liquid but there's also a thicker 'gel' type.

Grab Adhesives

These are supplied in cartridges for use with a skeleton gun, and take the form of a paste that you apply to one surface, and when you press the other item against it, it bonds instantly. Ideal for fixing skirting boards or dado rails, meaning screws and nails are not needed. Either water-based (non-smelling) or solvent-based (with a strong chemical aroma) and both are gap-filling. Again, beware of using cheap products, as some of these don't grip effectively – go for well-known makes, by old-established companies who have a reputation.

FIXINGS

Nails and screws work by the friction grip their shaft exerts on timber or another material's fibres that holds it in place. Masonry nails can grip on some plasters and soft bricks and blocks. Screws can be driven into a masonry wall via a circular plug in a pre-drilled hole, that expands when the screw enters, thus gripping the inside of the hole.

Nails

These range from 15cm (6in) wire nails, to tiny panel pins. Large 100–150mm (4–6in) nails are used in large-scale joinery, e.g. fixing floor joists and roof joists, while the majority of smaller sized nails might be used for fixing floorboards or outside for repairing a fence.

Screws

Screws are sold by shaft thickness denoted by a number (12 being almost the largest and 4 tiny) and length, so the edge of the box says, for instance, 10 × 50mm (2in), meaning thickness 10 and length 50mm (2in). 'Countersunk' means that the head fits into a corresponding depression drilled at the top of the hole when the screw is fully inserted, meaning you can fill above the head, and it's therefore invisible. 'Round-headed' means that the head of

the screw always sits on the surface. Hardly any woodscrews now have a single slot, the majority have a cross-shaped slot or a cross-shaped one with extra ridges. There are several names for these particular slots, which correspond to a particular screwdriver profile (plus drive, pozidrive, Philips). There are a variety of finishes, practically all are galvanized. Standard wood screws have the thread only part-way along their shaft, whereas chipboard or twinfast screws have thread all the way along, and can be used for all timbers.

An extremely useful type of screw that's recently become popular is the 'drywall' screw for fixing timbers, for use with an electric screwdriver or drill. Their tip is actually a timber-cutting drill, therefore allowing you to drill straight into the wood with no need for any 'clearance hole' to be drilled in one of the units to be fixed.

Attaching Things to a Wall

You can glue skirting boards and dado rails or other relatively light items to a wall, but for anything with weight, such as cupboards, bathroom fittings and WCs, you need to drill a hole in the wall and insert a suitable plug, into which you can put a screw. The plug is usually made of plastic, or metal for high-strength fixings, and designed so that when the screw enters its central hole, the material expands so that its circumference grips the inside of the hole in the masonry. Masonry nails sometimes grip when nailed into soft masonry, but when entering hard plasters or brick, they just snap. In the past, skirting boards were traditionally nailed to the wall, using chunky, long iron nails that were of rectangular cross-section; they are so large, that it's often difficult to remove old skirting boards without breaking them, because of these old nails.

The walls of most older houses are solid; however, newer properties can have hollow walls, i.e. there's a plasterboard outer surface covering a gap behind. There's a range of 'hollow wall fixings', mostly plastic, that work by being inserted through a hole and extending beyond the plasterboard panel, and expanding behind it when a screw is inserted. The screws are sold in tandem with the plugs as a kit, the screw's un-threaded shaft is designed to pass freely through the batten or material you're fixing, and the maximum thickness of this is called the 'maximum fixture thickness'.

Wall Plugs for Solid Walls

Plastic Plug for Brickwork and Blockwork
This standard wall plug has half its length cylindrical with profiled gripping lines, with its lower section split centrally, to permit girth expansion. The 'cluster' plug is similar, but incorporates a flange to stop it falling into a hole that is too deep.

Nylon Plug for Blockwork And Brickwork
Similar to the ordinary plug, but the split extends most of the way along the shaft. It has 'anti-rotation legs' that stick out at the centre of its length that give immediate grip.

*Frame Fixing for Fixing Doorframes and
Window Frames to Masonry*
This is a long nylon shaft, its upper majority being a smooth cylinder, the end part split to form an expanding plug. Its screw is threaded only at the end, since the remainder merely passes along the hole. The idea is that you drill one hole through both the timber of door or window frame, then continue drilling into the masonry (changing the drill bit to a masonry one). You next tap the long shaft into the hole completely. When you insert the screw, once it enters the expandable part that's in the masonry, it grips. Extremely useful, because you don't have to remove the doorframe to insert the masonry plug.

*Anchor Bolt/Wall Bolt for Fixing Heavy Timbers
such as Balustrades or Timbers to Support a Roof
Structure to Brickwork, Concrete or Stone*
A split, metal sleeve that encloses a strong bolt that has a tapering bulge at its end, held against the split. The shaft of the threaded bolt is arranged in such a way that when the sleeve is in a hole in the wall, and the other end of the bolt passes through the batten to be fixed, when the bolt is pulled against the item to be fixed by doing up a nut, the bulge inside the hole is pulled backwards against the split metal sleeve, progressively opening it up so that it grips firmly onto the inside of the hole.

Wall Plugs for Hollow Walls

Spring Toggle for Fixing to Plasterboard
This comprises a pair of springed metal 'wings'

Frame fixing plug (with one of its plastic wings broken off) and standard plastic wall plug.

hinged at a threaded nut, through which a long screw passes. You drill a relatively large hole in the plasterboard, pass the long screw through the item to be fixed, then screw the springed winged unit onto the end. Finally, you compress the metal wings back against the screw's shaft and push the end of the unit into the hole as far as you can. You hear the wings spring apart, then, when you screw the screw tight, the item to be fixed is drawn against the wall, and behind the plasterboard panel, the metal arms grip firmly to the board's reverse side, in effect introducing a large nut into this inaccessible area.

*Self-Drive, Made of Metal or Nylon, for Fixing
Lightweight Items to Plasterboard*
This is a tapering, pointed shaft with a helical screw thread on the outside, with special threaded screw that corresponds to a central nut accommodated within the unit. Using a large screwdriver, you insert this shaft directly into the plasterboard, allowing it to cut its own grip, without the need for pre-drilling. This effectively places a receptive 'nut' firmly inside the wall, so that you can then screw the item to it using the special screw.

Others
There is a range of other hollow-wall fittings, reliant on expansion of a plug behind the plasterboard panel; however, most of these are only suited to fixing lightweight items.

Spring toggle fixing.

CHAPTER 10

Insight Into the Trades

All the below trade federations have a 'Find a member' service on their websites, which also has further details on their activities.

CARPENTER/JOINER

Trade Association

The Institute of Carpenters (IOC) (www.institute-ofcarpenters.com; 0844 879 7696) was founded in 1890 and aims to promote excellence in the use of wood. It exists to support members who aspire to the highest standards of workmanship and professional conduct. They also work with

the craftsmen and women of tomorrow through their college membership programme. Membership of the institute is not restricted to carpenters but is also open to formwork carpenters, furniture and cabinet makers, boat builders (woodworking skills), joiners, shopfitters, heavy structural post-and-beam carpenters, wheelwrights, wood carvers and wood turners, in fact basically any craftsperson who works primarily with wood. The people listed on the 'Find a member' section of the website are current members of the institute and have demonstrated their competence by passing recognized craft examinations or by having undergone a

Carpenters' hand tools.

Carpenters' chisels and planes.

rigorous in-depth interview to determine the extent of their knowledge. The IOC advise that those using the site to locate craftsmen should ask for references and also satisfy themselves as to the person's competence.

(With thanks to Sharon Hutchings, of the IOC, who prepared the above.)

Overview

One of the most highly skilled trades, carpenters often specialize; for example, they might assemble or repair roof structures (the angles of the main timbers have to be cut very accurately, and these are mathematically calculated). Many roof structures are now factory-made, but these still have to be fitted, and some are still constructed *in situ*. Carpenters also fit doors and door frames, fit windows, and also lay floor joists and floorboards and construct and fit staircases. They can also be kitchen fitters, shopfitters, a separate trade all of its own: cabinets, work surfaces, glazing, etc., are usually prepared in a factory and fitted on site,

and made to precise details and tolerances. These craftsmen are likely to have knowledge of glazing, since window fitting tends to come under carpentry skills. Large timber joists are often nailed together; however, for smaller scale carpentry work timbers are more often glued and screwed: apart from large-scale joinery, nails tend to be used mostly for outside fencing and less accurate timber work. The trade is, therefore, subdivided into other trades within the carpentry profession, examples being cabinet-making, furniture designing/making, shopfitting, structural post-and-beam carpentry, wood-machining, wood-carving and turning, and general joinery work.

When timber-framed buildings were the norm, the carpenter was the most important of the building trades, and many extremely complicated joints were made in rock-hard oak, using adzes, cutting tools resembling an axe with its blade at right angles. A good carpenter should be able to splice (connect) new timber into an old timber structure for repairs, for instance, when repairing old timber windows; he should also be able to dismantle and rebuild timber structures, such as sash windows and shutters.

Some trades can be acquired to a limited extent by watching other people and years of practice, but carpentry is usually something that has to be taught and learnt.

PLUMBERS AND PLUMBING

Trade Associations

The Association of Plumbing and Heating Contractors (APHC) (www.competentpersonsscheme.co.uk; 0121 711 5030) is the leading trade association for the plumbing and heating industry in England and Wales. All member companies are qualified and professional businesses who are committed to high standards of workmanship and high levels of customer service. Search for a member in your area using the 'Find an APHC Installer' service on the website.

(With thanks to Nick Campion, press officer of the APHC, for preparing the above.)

The Chartered Institute of Plumbing and Heating Engineering (CIPHE) (www.ciphe.org.uk; 01708 472791) is the professional body for the UK plumbing and heating industry, founded 1906. Fifty active local branches are grouped within six areas.

Overview

Plumbing is normally the term describing the arrangement of pipework within your home for the distribution of drinking water and the removal of waterborne wastes, and also refers to the trade of working with such systems. It encapsulates the water supplies to and from the kitchen and bathroom, and also includes the central heating and the drainage system for all waste water. It also includes the guttering and downpipes that transport the water from the roof to the drainage system or a soakaway. Working with gas and gas appliances is also sometimes included in the term plumbing,

White Kuterlex: plastic-covered copper tubing. Yorkshire Copper Tube Ltd

however this is very much a specialist area and requires separate expertise, training and qualifications, and gas engineers have to be on the Gas Safe Register and can only undertake work in the areas upon which they have been assessed (*see below*). It is illegal for anyone unqualified to interfere with gas distribution systems.

Plumb of course refers to lead, and is the origin of the term, because originally lead pipes were used to transport water in the home, and in old houses you may still find these – steel pipes were also used (those built prior to 1960). Nowadays copper and plastic are the materials used, and plastic pipes can also be used for hot water and central heating systems. Plumbing work, and plumbers' training, breaks down into five key areas: hot and cold drinking water supplies, central heating, gas installation work, lead and copper roofing and sanitation/drainage.

Beware of amateur plumbers who may charge less than a fully trained person: as well as doing unreliable work they may do things that contravene the water authority regulations. A new boiler has to meet certain energy efficiency requirements

and the installation has to be registered with the local authority.

Pipes

In older pre-1960 properties you may find lead and mild steel pipes, but modern plumbing pipes are copper and plastic. Plastic water-supply pipes are joined by simply pushing them into a coupling joint (straight, right-angled or tee) to make a perfectly waterproof joint. Copper pipes can now also be joined using push-fit joints, or they can be joined using solder joints or compression fittings: the latter is where the pipe and the fitting are joined by progressively tightening a nut against a collar within the fitting, an action that compresses a metal ring (olive) around the pipe, effecting a seal. Copper and plastic pipes are compatible. Kuterlex is copper tube coated with a seamless plastic cover, which protects the copper tube against aggressive materials. It is colour-coded to identify the services in accordance with UK local authority specifications and British Standards regulations.

Plastic waste pipes are of a considerably larger diameter than supply pipes, and are joined either

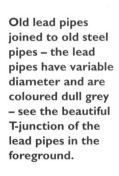

Old lead pipes joined to old steel pipes – the lead pipes have variable diameter and are coloured dull grey – see the beautiful T-junction of the lead pipes in the foreground.

House stopvalve between sections of lead pipe.

Metal downpipe of an old WC pan coupled to a modern plastic high-level cistern.

by compression fittings, on the same principle as copper compression fittings (the difference being that rubber washers are compressed to make the seal), by using special adhesive or via push-fit fittings. Old lead piping is dull grey or may be painted, and usually has an irregular diameter and sweeping curves, bulging joints and junctions. Scraping the surface reveals a bright shiny silvery appearance. Mild steel pipe is usually black and of constant diameter with partial threading evident at joints. Ancient pipes are often painted to match the walls.

Cold-Water Supply

Pressurized cold water is termed potable (suitable for drinking) water, and is delivered to your house through the 'communications pipe' under the road and leads to the water company stopvalve, which is usually about 750mm (30in) below ground level under a hinged or circular push-fit lid in the pavement. The pipe on the other side of this stopvalve is called the 'service pipe' and enters your house through foundations. Inside the home there is the house stopvalve, that controls the water flow; on

Copper piping.

newer houses, or if the water company has made changes, there may be a water meter incorporated in the supply pipe, either outside under the accessible chamber where the company stopvalve is, or possibly within the building. Nowadays the standard supply pipe is made of 25mm (1in) plastic (polyethylene), coloured blue, whereas in the past this supply pipe might have been made of plastic, copper, galvanized steel or lead. The stopvalve in your house is likely to be in one of the following locations: under the kitchen sink, in a downstairs toilet, understairs cupboard, garage or basement or under a wooden floorboard just inside the front door.

The water company stopvalve should not be turned off by anyone other than a water authority official or a professional plumber, since legally it is owned by the company; practical reasons for this can be because it may control the flow to other properties as well as your own, and also there's the danger you may damage it, especially if it is old and fragile.

House mains stopvalve connected to copper pipe and blue mains water delivery pipe.

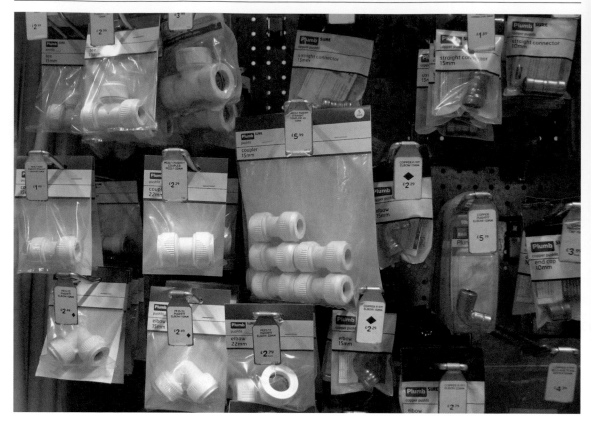

Plastic pushfit plumbing pipe-connection fittings. B&Q

Pressurized cold water delivered to your house is controlled by taps and valves. Turning a tap's handle allows a rubber washer to progressively block or release pressure from the open end of the water-delivery pipe. A cistern valve, such as in a WC or tank in the loft, operates in the same way, except that it is the lifting action of a floating plastic ball (or bell-shaped plastic device) on the water's surface that activates the water-blocking mechanism. Delivery of water is governed by water supply (water fittings) regulations.

A 'direct' cold-water supply is where all the cold-water outlet points (i.e. taps or feeds to appliances) are fed directly from the main supply and are therefore safe to drink. An 'indirect' water supply is where only the kitchen-sink cold-tap (and a water softener, if used) and the cold-water storage cistern is connected to the main, and the other outlets in the house are fed from this cistern, which is usually situated in the loft; for older systems it is

recommended that you should not drink this water, as there's the possibility of contamination from the storage tank; however, modern storage systems have safety features. A modified cold-water supply is a combination of direct and indirect, whereby several cold-water outlets are fed from the main, while others are fed from the storage tank. Prior to 1980 most systems were indirect, whereas they are not so now. Very old storage tanks were made of steel, which always eventually corroded so that few are left, and plastic tanks have been in use for thirty-five years. All cisterns fitted since 1991 incorporate a tight-fitting lid and filtered overflow to ensure that insects cannot enter.

Above-Ground Drainage

Waste water flows along pipes beneath sinks, baths and behind/below WCs, and there is always a U-shaped bend in the outlet pipe that forms a water seal or trap, to separate the foul air within

RIGHT: **Waste trap to be installed under a bath or sink.** B&Q

BELOW: **Above ground grey foul-water drainage pipes.** B&Q

the drain from that within your home. Water flows via gravity along pipes to go outside to join the soil vent or stack-pipe, and from here to pipes below ground. In the past, waste water from basins did not mix with foul waste from WCs until the two mixed outside underground, whereas now it is usual for water from basins to connect straight to the main stack pipe, to which WCs are also connected. The large-diameter plastic stack-pipe used above ground is always grey-coloured (unless painted), whereas the same diameter plastic waste-pipe used underground is always brown. Very old stack-pipes were made of metal.

Below-Ground Drainage

'Surface water' is that from the roof going down gutters, 'foul water' is from a WC and 'waste water' is from a basin, bath or sink. Discharge pipes go underground and meet the main sewer at an inspection chamber, accessible via a lid, so that it can be accessed to clear blockages. Sink waste-pipes in older properties might lead to a gulley that has a trap, from here a pipe leads to the inspection chamber, where the waste water is mixed with the

Below ground (brown) foul-water drainage pipes. B&Q

foul water from WCs. From the inspection chamber the liquid travels along a pipe to the main sewer. All sewer pipes are now made of brown plastic but in the past, vitrified clay pipes joined in sections were used. Repair is a specialist job, as the broken section has to be cut out and replaced. Glazed vitrified clay (used until the late-1960s and 1970s) is the oldest type: it has a glazed surface and was laid in 1m (3ft) sections, jointed by sockets whose collar was filled with a cement mortar mix. Vitrified clay is the more modern form of clay pipe, with a smooth matt finish and black polypropylene couplings for the sections, which are about 160cm (5ft) long.

Emergency Shut-Off

If You Have an Emergency Pipe Burst in Your Cold-Water System:
Close the stopvalve in the house and, if you have a cold-water storage tank, turn on all cold taps – this allows water in the tank to drain. If you can find a gatevalve (with a red circular handle) below the storage tank, close this too.

For a Burst in the Hot-Water System:
Turn off the boiler or allow fire to go out in a solid fuel boiler, and if you have a DHW storage cylinder, turn off the gatevalve on the pipe at its bottom. Otherwise turn off the main stop valve, which will have the same effect, but you may have to wait for the cold-water storage tank to drain.

If You Have a Burst in the Central Heating System:
Turn off the boiler or allow the fire to go out in a solid fuel boiler, then turn off the main stopvalve or else the valve controlling entry of water to the central heating overflow tank, if there is one. Then drain the central heating system at the drain cock, which you should find at its lowest point, possibly outside the house – if it is inside the house, connect a hose to the outside for drainage.

Below ground and above ground drainage pipes in position before the trench is filled.

Hot-Water Supply

Water is heated by a water heater (usually a boiler), which either heats it as required (termed a 'multipoint' or 'combination' boiler) or delivers it to a coil of piping – a heat exchanger – within an enclosed Domestic Hot Water (DHW) storage cylinder, from where hot taps are fed from the surrounding water, fed from the top of this cylinder (water enters at the bottom). Water can also be heated via an electric immersion heater within the DHW storage cylinder: this works on the same principle as an electric kettle element on a large scale. The multipoint boiler simply heats hot water as required and it is drawn off via hot taps, whereas the combination boiler also heats the water for central heating, separately. There can also be a gas or electric single point water heater above a sink or basin.

The heating water that feeds the heat exchanger within the DHW storage cylinder either rises via natural gravity – called gravity circulation – or utilizes a circulation pump, termed a 'fully pumped system', the latter being the standard method used today. The hot-water outlet is at top, with the cold-water feed at the bottom.

Possible Plumbing Disasters

Cold-Water Storage Tank Corrosion, Leakage
An old, metallic water-tank inevitably corrodes and it's reasonably straightforward to replace it with the equivalent-sized plastic tank. You may need to cut the old metal tank into pieces to get it out of a small loft hatch.

Leaks from Corroded Pipes
If these are in the loft or under floorboards upstairs, they can cause problems, possibly damaging or destroying ceilings. Emergency action is to first turn off the water and a boiler, then if you have a cold-water storage tank in the loft, also turn on all the taps: remember a considerable amount

of water is stored here, enough to do damage if not drained quickly through taps. There may also be a stopcock below the cold-water storage tank, which you can also turn off.

Burst Delivery Pipe Underground

This rarely happens, however ground movement or corrosion might cause it. If the burst is to the street side of the company's stopvalve, then repair is the water company's responsibility, whereas if it is to the house side it is yours. There are many insurance schemes run by the water companies, offering repair of such pipes in an emergency.

Soil Pipe Leaking Underground

Old, clay pipes can crack for various reasons and, if you suspect this, have a CCTV survey done to establish the facts. Cure is either a question of excavating the broken section and replacing it, or sometimes you can have the pipes relined from the inside by specialist firms. Sometimes tree roots can grow into drains, in which case your house insurance might cover the cost of repair. What is not covered by insurance policies is wear and tear, and breaking through age: check the situation with your insurance company in the first instance. Installation of new underground sewer pipes, or alteration of old ones, has to be done in accordance with Approved Document H of the building regulations, but repairs don't have to be. However, your builder

---

Expert Quote

Ken Milbery, master plumber and proprietor of the Plumbwell shops (01689 848822 and 020 8684 7007):

As a general rule you find that underground sewers run at the front or back of the house for the whole street. This therefore means that if you have a WC at any exterior wall of the house, you're only going to have to make one right-angled turn to direct the waste to the drains. At every underground change of sewer pipe direction you have to have an inspection chamber, and for drainage you need a 1 in 40 drop. Vital advice is always to find out where your main stopcock/stopvalve is and to make sure it works.

---

should probably consult your local authority Building Control department, to have it checked to make sure the repair is done correctly before filling in the excavations.

Collapsing Metal Guttering

Old, cast-iron guttering is heavy enough to kill someone if it falls, so it's vital to make sure it's

Licence No. **3456789**

Name
Patrick Brian Glover
Company
Glover & Sons
Gas Installers

Registration No. **123456**

Valid from   **01/04/2011**

Expires   **31/03/2012**

To confirm the validity of this card please contact Gas Safe Register on: **0800 408 5500** or online at: **www.GasSafeRegister.co.uk** If this card is found please return to Gas Safe Register, PO Box 6804, Basingstoke, RG24 4NB

Gas safe register sample identity card. (Gas Safe Register does not endorse the information or illustrations within this publication.)
Gas Safe Register

securely fitted or replaced if it is dangerously corroded. Either replace all of it with modern plastic guttering, or you can buy new cast-iron guttering, but this is expensive and the whole lot will have to be replaced. Some listed buildings may require the use of matching cast-iron guttering for replacement.

GAS ENGINEERS

Gas Safe Register

The Gas Safe Register (www.gassaferegister.co.uk; 0800 408 5500) is the official list of gas engineers who are qualified to work safely and legally on gas appliances. By law, all gas engineers must be on the Gas Safe Register. It replaced CORGI. Only use a Gas Safe registered engineer to fit, fix or service your appliances, and always check the engineer's Gas Safe Register ID card on both sides, to make sure the person is qualified for the work you need; also contact the Gas Safe register to make sure the person is registered with them. For more information and to find and check an engineer contact the above.

Gas valve – turn it one-quarter turn to cut off gas supply, in-line with the pipe means gas is switched on.

If You Are a Landlord
(The following is copyright of the Gas Safe Register.)

Landlords are legally responsible for the safety of their tenants. Landlords should make sure maintenance and annual safety checks on gas appliances are carried out by a Gas Safe registered engineer.
   By law landlords must make sure:

- Pipework, appliances and flues provided for tenants are maintained in a safe condition.
- That all appliances and flues that they provide for tenants have an annual safety check.
- That maintenance and annual safety checks are carried out by an engineer registered with the Gas Safe register.
- All gas equipment (including any appliance left by a previous tenant) is safe or otherwise removed before re-letting.
- A gas safety record is provided to the tenant within 28 days of completing the check or to any new tenant before they move in.
- They keep a copy of the gas safety record for two years.

(With thanks to Rachel Boon of the Gas Safe Register.)

HEATING AND HEATING ENGINEERING

Trade Association

The APHC (see above), also HETAS for certain heating appliances (see below).

Overview

The first medieval heating system was a log fire positioned centrally in the main room of the house, with a hole in the roof through which smoke escaped. In the sixteenth century fireplaces were developed, and a large inglenook fireplace would take up an entire wall, incorporating a massive overhead beam (bressummer) supporting the brickwork above and there could be seats in the fireplace area, as well as bread ovens near the source of heat. Fireplaces generally became slightly smaller over the years, burning coal instead of logs. Central heating, as we know it today, was a Victorian invention, with radiators made of ornately decorated cast iron and displaying very obtrusive pipework.

Types of Heating

Central heating describes an overall system throughout the house, as opposed to individual fires used for each room. The most usual type is 'wet' central heating, utilizing constantly circulating water and radiators or underfloor pipes. 'Dry' central heating is normally electric heat-storage radiators (running on an economy tariff) or, less commonly, heated air is delivered to vents near the floorboards or some underfloor heating (UFH) is via electrically heated elements.

Wet Central Heating

This is where water is electrically pumped from the boiler, where it is heated, to metal radiators or underfloor pipes and back again in a circular flow. As the temperature of the surface of these vessels cools, because of the colder surrounding atmosphere, the internal water is replaced by heated water from the boiler. Piping is hidden beneath floorboards, inside solid floors, chased into the thickness of walls or mounted on the wall or skirting-board surface. The temperature can be adjusted by a single thermostat for the whole house or individually at each radiator, using thermostatic radiator valves (TRVs). Heating is switched on by activating the electric pump, usually managed by a pre-programmable control panel near the boiler. Radiators were originally made of cast iron, are now usually of steel, with the most efficient being of aluminium; there are also 'skirting radiators' that replace skirting boards.

Most systems have 'the two-pipe system', whereby two pipes join the boiler, one for the water to be delivered to the network of radiators around the house – the 'flow' – and the other to return the cooled water the boiler – the 'return'. Normally a circulating pump pumps the water around the boiler and radiators. In very old properties you might find a 'gravity circulation' system. In this antiquated and inefficient system lighter hot water rises and colder, heavier, water sinks, the idea being that water flows along the entire system by gravity. Gravity circulation systems are definitely outdated and need replacing, and are often associated with solid fuel heaters.

The boiler normally also heats the hot water, but this water circuit is separate from that of the central heating. A sealed system is where the water is supplied to fill the system directly from the main cold water supply, and sealed within the heating circuit, therefore not under the influence of atmospheric pressure – a sealed system is slightly pressurized and needs to operate at the boiler manufacturer's recommended pressure; if the pressure is too low, you can raise the pressure by allowing more water into the system by temporarily opening a tap, and if pressure it too high, you have to drain some water from the system. A 'vented' central heating system utilizes a feed and expansion tank and works in a different way.

Underfloor Central Heating (UFH)

Wet UFH heating is achieved by water-carrying radiator pipes beneath the floor's surface, which can be concrete, flagstones, tiles or floorboards, causing the entire floor to act as a radiator. Dry underfloor heating is a system or electrical elements laid beneath the floor that work in the same way. UFH is extremely good for traditionally cold surfaces, such as slate or stone, and is ideal for drying up water spills in bathrooms.

Open Fires

These are often used as a top-up to central heating. Their function is to give off heat, direct smoke up the chimney and not create unacceptable draughts. Fireplace fitters should be registered with HETAS (see Chapter 7). Fireplaces are either of stone construction or a combination of cast-iron, marble or stone back panel with a mantelpiece made of other materials. All have a metal support for the combustible material, a grate, which permits air flow beneath the fire.

Stoves

Stoves developed as a more efficient type of heating than an open fire, the idea being to give off heat from the outer casing, which can be cast-iron or ceramic; they can sometimes incorporate a back boiler for central heating. Swedish-style stoves have a large and decorative surface area of ceramic tiling. Stoves are either wood-burning, multi-fuel (smokeless fuel, coal or timber) or gas-fired. Glass doors enclose the firebox and there's usually a cast-iron

stovepipe that sends smoke up the chimney. Fitters should be HETAS registered, (see Chapter 7).

Gas Fires

These can mimic solid-fuel fires and, like the above, are often used as top-up to central heating. They can either be a radiant heater (living flame type) that is a burner unit, or a convector fire, where air is drawn in from underneath and, after being heated by the fire, dissipated at the top. Again, fitters should be HETAS registered (see Chapter 7).

ELECTRIC WIRING

Trade Associations

The NICEIC (www.niceic.com; 0870 013 0382), set up in the 1950s, is the UK electrical contracting industry's independent voluntary regulatory body assessing the competence of UK electricians. Over 25,000 contractors are registered with them, and there's a 'Find a contractor service' on their website, as well as a 'Wall of shame', listing electrical contractors who claim to be members, but are not.

The Electrical Contractors Association (ECA) (www.eca.co.uk; 020 7313 4800), founded in 1901, is the UK's leading trade association representing the interests of contractors who design, install, inspect, test and maintain electrical and electronic equipment and services. 'Representing the best in electrical engineering and building services'.

Overview

Working on anything to do with electricity is always a job for experts, and you should never tamper with electrical wiring or sockets unless you are qualified to do so. Every year around 12,500 house fires, 750 serious injuries and 10 deaths are caused by unsafe electrics in the home. Furthermore, since 2005 an electrical safety law, Part P of the Building Regulations, was introduced. This brings electrical work in the home under statutory control, and means that only an electrician registered with a government-approved scheme (such as operated by NICEIC) should carry out the majority of electrical work in the home; because such a registered individual is deemed a 'competent person', the local authority building control department does not need to inspect their work afterwards. After completion of

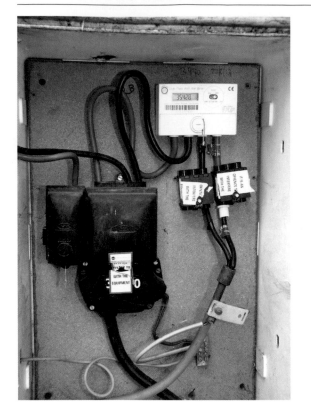

the work, the registered electrician will issue you with an electrical safety certificate and a Compliance Certificate to confirm it meets the requirements of the building regulations. To comply with the law, if you do certain electrical jobs yourself, you must notify your local building control department before you start, and pay the appropriate fee for them to inspect the work afterwards. It is a criminal offence to carry out work that does not comply with the building regulations, with a maximum fine of £5,000. Furthermore, you won't know if the work is safe (with the attendant risk of fire or electrocution), the lack of certification may cause problems when you come to sell your house and building control may insist you have the work redone.

Some electrical work is classified as 'minor' and does not necessarily have to be undertaken by a professionally qualified person or be inspected afterwards – one example being replacing a light-fitting in certain circumstances; however, you should always contact your local building control department, or a qualified electrician, to find out what you are, and are not, allowed to do. Crucially, this

ABOVE: **Electricity company main fuses and meter – never ever tamper with these.**

LEFT: **Electricity mains consumer unit, meter and company fuse.**

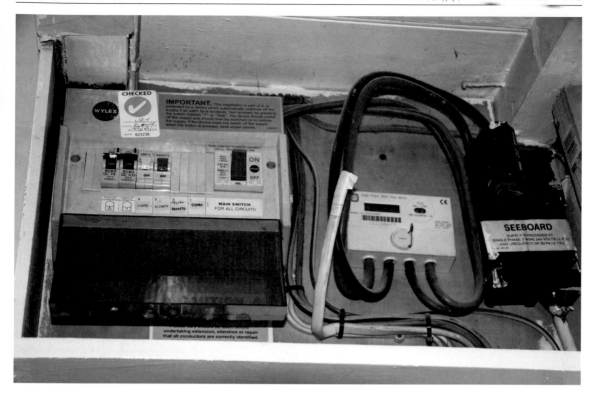

ABOVE: **Electricity main consumer unit, meter and company fuse.**

BELOW: **Old fashioned fuse box.**

'minor' work must comply with BS 7671, the wiring regulations, so the recommendation is: never ever tamper with electrical wiring unless you are qualified to do so. Kitchens, bathrooms and gardens are classified as 'special locations' because the risk of electrical shock is greater, and here almost all electrical work should be done by a professionally qualified person.

BS 7671 requires that persons undertaking electrical installation work should be 'competent' and it's a legal requirement that all installations or additions must be tested and inspected by a competent person using appropriate test equipment. One thing to bear in mind is, if money is tight, much electrical work is non specialist; for instance, chasing out channels in walls, raising floorboards (however, raising floorboards in the vicinity of old wiring can be dangerous). You might be able to find an agreeable electrician who is prepared to let you do this non-specialist work, leaving him to do the wiring and connections, thus reducing his working time.

If you're buying an old house and a full structural survey is performed, the surveyor should put in his report if an electrical safety check needs to be carried out. You can look for danger signs (*see below*) and commission an electrical safety check anyway for peace of mind. A proper electrical survey ideally should be done in all houses every ten years.

Making sure that your electrical wiring is safe is absolutely vital, because hazardous old wiring and equipment can cause fires in unseen places, e.g. under the floorboards or in an understairs cupboard; in fact 10 per cent of home fires are electrical, and a third of these are directly attributable to outdated or bad wiring. And if your home insurance could prove that you were aware that your home's wiring was faulty or outdated and didn't rectify it, they might have grounds for dismissing any claim. Never ever touch any part of un-tested electrical equipment, such as casings for old fuse boxes or ancient wiring, as this could cause electrocution and death.

Theory and Practice

Electric current is a flow of electrically charged particles that travels to your home via sheathed wiring, two cables that must be separated by their insulating sheathing. If the insulating sheathing fails and the two bare wires touch each other there's a dangerous reaction called a short circuit, which results in a bang and flash, possibly also sparks. If this happens, a protective device, such as a miniature circuit breaker (MCB), residual current device (RCD) or, in older homes, a fuse, will detect the fault and automatically interrupt the flow of power. If this safety mechanism fails, for whatever reason, a fire can possibly result, because of the sparking caused by the current flow between the two wires. If an electrical appliance is faulty, the same reaction may occur.

Two single wire cables enter the house, one of which is connected to the company's sealed service fuse, beyond which is the meter. From here cables run to the main consumer unit (originally called the fuse box), which contains a number of miniature circuit breakers (MCBs), (or fuses, in older homes), each one of which controls a different 'wiring circuit' within the house. From the consumer unit are a number of cables going to different parts of the building, each one being a different wiring circuit: one may control downstairs power sockets, another the upstairs lighting, another the kitchen circuits and so on. Each circuit is governed by its MCB, or fuse, of a suitable size. Because of this, if there's a problem, only one MCB trips or fuse blows, and only one section of the electricity system goes down. Modern MCBs often trip when a lightbulb blows and, if this is the only cause, can be safely switched on again. In all other cases, the reason why the fuse or MCB has been operated must be cured before the power is switched on again. There are also individual cartridge-type fuses within electrical plugs, which automatically cut off the power if the appliance is faulty; the rating, in amps, of these fuses should be tailored to the appliance it is fitted to: new appliances already have plugs fitted with the correct fuse inside.

In the vicinity of the company's main fuse there is also a third wire (connected to other cables) coming from outside the house, called the earth or ground connection. This cable often used to be attached to the lead water-pipe or steel gas-pipe, now it's more usual to have it connected to an earth spike that's driven straight down into the soil itself outside the house. Only a qualified electrician can judge if this vital 'earth' connection, connected to various items within the home, is functioning

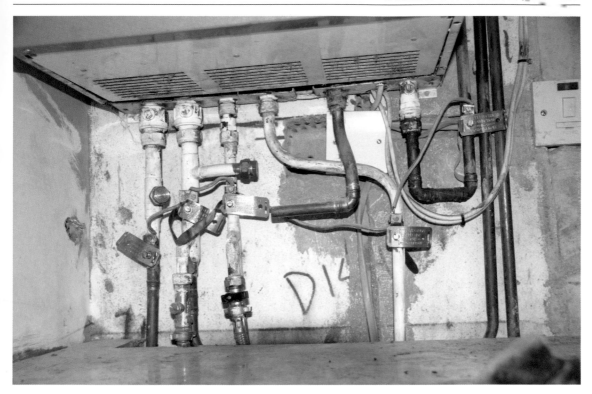

Earth bonding onto a number of pipes below a boiler.

Signs That a House's Electrical Wiring or Main Equipment Needs Urgent Attention or Replacement

- Cables anywhere that are coated in black rubber (phased out in the 1960s), or any signs of fabric or cotton insulation (pre-1950s). However, there is a new type of silk-covered cable for antique lighting that is perfectly safe: only a qualified electrician can decide.
- Fuse box with a wooden back, or made of cast iron or ceramic.
- Round-pin sockets.
- Round-shaped light sockets, unless these are specially made modern 'antique' fittings.
- Original Bakelite light switches or lampholders.
- Electrical power sockets mounted on skirting boards.
- Non-approved light fittings in a bathroom.

Danger signs that should never be ignored:

- Brown burn marks on plastic or wood.
- Buzzing sounds.
- Hot sockets, switches or plugs, or flickering lights.
- Frequently tripping MCBs or blowing fuses for no apparent reason.

Master plasterer and builder Michael Bell giving a final perfect coat of finish plaster to a wall.

correctly. Legally, certain metallic items within the home have to be connected to earth, and only a qualified electrician can tell you if the correct connections have been made.

OTHER TRADE ORGANIZATIONS, ALL WITH 'FINDER SERVICES' ON THEIR WEBSITES

Plastering

Federation of Plastering and Drywall Contractors (FPDC) (www.fpdc.org; 020 7634 9480). National trade association with both specialist contractor and associate members that are involved in designing and installing internal and external build solutions. Covering specialist contractors in the following: traditional solid plastering, fibrous plastering, basic plastering, roughcast, render and external wall insulation, screeding, drywall construction, suspended ceilings and steel frame systems. This is a members' organization, and is not consumer-led.

Double-Glazing

Glass and Glazing Federation (GGF) (www.ggf.org.uk; 0207 939 9101). Trade association representing companies who make, supply or fit, glass and glass-related products. The primary representative organization for companies involved in all aspects of the manufacture of plate glass and products and services for all types of glazing in commercial and domestic sectors. Over half the installations performed in the UK are carried out by GGF members.

Fenestration Self-Assessment Scheme (FENSA) (www.fensa.co.uk; 020 7645 3700). The leading body providing homeowners' protection in the double-glazing industry for windows and doors. By using a FENSA-registered company, you get a 5–10 year insurance-backed guarantee and a FENSA Building Regulations certificate as proof of compliance with the current building regulations. It was set up by the GGF to allow registered companies to self-certify that their installations comply with current building regulations.

Glossary

Abutment Edge of roof abutting wall or chimney.

Acrow Prop/Screw Jack Supportive metal pole, of adjustable height.

Air-Brick Perforated brick, used to allow ventilation, most often to under-floor areas. A variation on using an actual brick is a sturdy metal plate made as a honeycomb of holes, which is either double-brick or single-brick sized.

Anobium punctatum Common furniture beetle or woodworm.

Anticoagulant Poison Rodent poison that prevents blood forming clots, causing death.

Anti-Dry-Rot Paint Chemical preservative paint that protects timber and masonry surfaces from being attacked by the dry rot fungus.

Apron Metal flashing at the front side of chimney-stack where it emerges from roof.

Area Flood Defences Actions taken by central and local government to protect property.

Artex Texturing compound for putting a surface on ceilings.

ASUC Association of Specialist Underpinning Contractors.

Back Hearth Area under an open fire, normally made of firebricks or concrete.

Ballast Mixture of sand and small stones (aggregate) that can be mixed with cement to make concrete.

Ballvalve Float-operated valve used to control the flow of water into a tank or WC cistern.

Bargeboard Wooden board fixed beneath the verge edge of tiles, decorative bargeboards were a feature of Victorian houses.

Battens Sticks or laths of timber nailed horizontally along the roof structure's surface, on which tiles or slates hang, or to which they are nailed.

Binder A substance that is mixed with sand that, when activated by water, bonds the sand particles together to create a solid material, such as mortar, that sticks to bricks or stone.

Blown (Tiles) When tiles delaminate and separate into their component layers.

Blown Brick When the outer rain repellent 'fireskin' of the brick has broken down, allowing entry of water and consequent brick decay.

Blown Plaster When old plaster has lost its adherence to the substrata. In itself this is no problem, but once part is removed, it's difficult to make an effective repair.

Boiler   Device powered by gas, oil, liquid petroleum gas or solid fuel, for heating water. All boilers are now condensing boilers, whereas in the past they were not of this type. There are basically two types: a combination (combi) boiler, which provides heating and hot water directly from the boiler, requiring no hot-water storage cylinder; while a regular (conventional) boiler heats the central heating directly and produces hot water to heat a DHW storage cylinder.

Bonnet Tiles   External corner tiles, shaped for covering the hips or ridges of roofs.

Break-Back Trap   Mouse trap or the larger rat trap. Baited rodent-killing device that utilizes a trip for a spring, triggered when the animal presses on a lever to reach the bait.

Brickie   Bricklayer.

Brief   Client's description of work to be done.

Builder's Opening   Wall opening at the base of a chimney into which an open fire is installed.

Building Regulations   Controls administered by the local authority to regulate the technical aspects of building and quality of construction and workmanship.

Camp Ceiling   Attic-type ceiling that follows the line of rafters at the sides and the collar beam horizontally above.

Canopy   Shaped hood attached to the flue for gathering smoke.

Capillary Action   Where water is sucked upwards or inwards from a damp place to a drier part of the structure.

Capsheet   The mineral finished 'top sheet' type of roofing felt, to be applied as the final layer.

Catnic   Colloquial term (relating to the company that makes them) for a relatively lightweight, steel, boxed beam, constructed to act as a lintel.

Cavity   The gap between twin walls of cavity wall constructions, normally around 50mm (2in) wide.

Cavity Drain Membrane   A dimple-backed plastic membrane for damp-proofing walls. The dimples create a cavity for water's drainage.

Certificate of Structural Adequacy   Vital document you must ask for after subsidence remedial work has been done on a property.

Chimney   Surrounding structure to direct smoke to the open air, terminating at a pot, cowl or other fitting.

Chippings   Pieces of hard mineral, usually green or white, either incorporated in the final roofing felt layer or added separately as a way of protecting the top layer of felt.

Chippy   Carpenter.

Clean Storage Job   Boarding over a loft space for storage purposes only.

Coade Stone   Unique fired material that was developed by Mrs Eleanor Coade in 1769, used to make architectural features on buildings as well as statuary: it is a warm golden beige colour and has a slightly shiny surface.

'Coffin' Tank   Colloquial term for long narrow water tank laid lengthways, designed for space saving.

Cold-Water Storage Tank/Main Water Cistern   Large tank situated at a high place (usually the roof space), to accommodate a considerable amount of cold water, for distribution throughout the house at reasonable pressure, due to its physically high position.

Collars/Collar Beams   Beams fixed horizontally to rafters (between purlins) at around chest height.

Common Rafters Relatively unusual timbers that support roof battens and tiles. Found only in old properties, often when the rafter span is split into two lengths, the common rafters added on behind the purlins.

Conservation Area Area designated by the local authority as being 'of special architectural or historic interest, that the character of which it is desirable to preserve or enhance'.

Contract Document itemizing requirements that the builder and client must agree to.

Creep (Lead) When lead gets old and spreads, becoming thinner.

Crown Post Vertically placed timber supporting the middle of collar beams, found in medieval constructions.

Damp-Proof Course (DPC) A continuous layer of waterproof material installed in a wall at low level, serving to block groundwater's upward passage to drier brick or stonework. Originally a double layer of slate, later a rubber-based plastic material. These were only mandatory after The Public Health Act of 1875.

Damp-Proof Membrane (DPM) Heavy-grade building polythene, installed in floors to prevent moisture's upward movement.

Dead Bond When a brick (or stone) structure that's joined to another with mortar develops a crack or general breakdown that compromises the effectiveness of the bond, potentially causing a hazard, such as a chimney-stack that can be blown down in high wind.

Deck/Decking The timber sheet material (normally exterior-grade plywood) used to make the flat timber covering that is nailed to the firrings above the roof joists.

Defective Work Faults that appear after completion.

Defects Liability Period The period after work's termination during which problems are corrected under contract before release of a retained payment.

Devil's Coat Bonding coat of plaster that's been scored (scratched) in preparation for applying tiles.

Differential Settlement This is when settlement affects only a part of a building, e.g. a new addition, and may mean that the new foundations move relative to those of the original house.

Dob and Dab Method of affixing plasterboard to a wall's surface, whereby special bonding adhesive is applied in localized spots of the wall or plasterboard back side, prior to pushing it against the wall to bond. The adhesive is gap-filling allowing you to 'lose' space in an uneven wall.

Domestic Hot-Water Cylinder The fully lagged copper tank, usually in a bathroom/utility room, that is designed to store heated water.

Dormer Window A gabled structure protruding from the roof slope with sides (cheeks) and a window at the front.

Double-Vacuum Treated Method of pre-treating timber so as to preserve it from attack by fungi and rot.

Drain Cock Valve that incorporates a nozzle for fitting a hose to, facilitating the draining down of a DHW cylinder or heating system.

Dressings Rows of stones or bricks used to surround openings in a wall – notably in flint buildings.

Dry Lining Process of creating a separated dry surface in front of the original damp wall. This can be moisture-proofed plasterboard mounted on polythene-clad wooden timbers, or wet plaster applied to a special expanded metal lath. Often used when waterproofing basements and cellars.

Dry Pack   Extremely dry-mix mortar, specified for strength.

Dust   Cement.

Dwarf Wall   Miniature wall, built to facilitate a loft-conversion, that links the roof structure with the RSJ support beneath.

Eaves   Bottom edge of roof, usually referring to the edge of tiles or slates.

Energy Management System (EMA)   Electronic device for controlling the boiler, turning on/off hot water and central heating.

Estimate   The builder's assessment of the approximate cost (bear in mind that other factors only apparent after the job has begun may increase the cost).

Euophyrum confine   Wood-boring weevil.

Event, Event Year   A surge of insurance claims within a limited period that is all attributable to one cause, e.g. flooding or subsidence.

False Ashlaring   Where stucco is used to render a wall's surface and scored to make it look like blocks of stone.

Fascia Board   Horizontal board fixed underneath eaves on to which guttering is attached.

Fireback   Back lining to a builder's opening, to protect the masonry.

Firring Strip   The long, tapering, softwood timbers that are nailed on top of, or across, the roof joists, below the decking, to give the required slope for directing water to the gutter end of a flat roof.

First Fix   The first jobs to be done in a newly built house.

Fish Plate   Steel plate, used in pairs and bolted each side of a timber joint, to add strength.

Fittings   Collective term for ridge tiles, metal castings, or hip tiles that fit over and bridge two planes of a roof's tiled or slated surface.

Flashing   Waterproof strip, usually of lead, used to bridge and cover junctions between disparate building elements, for example a chimney-stack rising up through a roof.

Flashings   Strips of moulded lead or other material, used to weatherproof the gaps between dissimilar materials – for instance between roof tiles or slates and a chimney.

Flaunching   The mortar used to bond the base of a chimney to a pot or else the mortar used to bridge the gap between a roof and chimney.

Flitch Plate   Steel plate slotted into the thickness of timber to reinforce it or to strengthen it.

Flood Pack/Kit   Emergency equipment required, to be assembled prior to its use.

Flood Plan   Plan of action formulated before any flood is anticipated.

Flood Resilience   Measures to make the fabric and services of a building more robust and easier to clean, dry out and reinstate in the event of floodwater getting inside the building.

Flood Resistance   Measures taken to protect property from flooding – the whole building perimeter needs to be resistant.

Flood-Risk Assessment   The Environment Agency's way of compiling information about the hazards and types of risks that a flood presents.

Flood Risk   The likelihood of flooding and the possible damage a flood could do – affects both use of building and its insurance cover. You need to know the probability of flooding and its likely severity.

Flue   A passageway within a chimney for conducting smoke.

Flue Liner Something added to inside of a chimney to form a continuous gas-proof surface.

Flue Pipe Metal pipe used to connect an appliance to the flue.

Fogging The professional process of applying large quantities of insecticide to an area.

Footings/Foundations Courses of underground bricks or strips of concrete laid directly onto the earth below ground, forming the foundations.

Frass The powder left behind after an attack from wood-boring insects.

French Drain Layer of shingle in an excavated trench at a wall's base, that facilitates the draining away of rain at the base of the wall.

Gable End Triangular wall beneath the sides of a pitched roof.

Gatevalve Control tap for low-pressure water, e.g. on an exit from a cold-water storage tank; it has a wheel-like red control knob.

Gauge The spacing of courses of tiles or slates, and their fixing battens.

Green Applied to new brickwork, plaster and new timber. Meaning fresh, full of water, not fully cured or dried out sufficiently.

Gulley Grid-covered outside drain that discharges to main drains, incorporating a water-filled trap.

Handler/Claims Manager The person who deals with insurance claims on behalf of the company, normally a loss adjuster, and sometimes a structural engineer or building surveyor.

Hearth A 'construction hearth' is the main section, beneath the 'superimposed hearth' or top surface.

Heat Exchanger The arrangement of pipes inside the domestic hot water cylinder, inside which hot water is constantly circulating to and from the boiler in order to heat the surrounding water.

Heave The opposite of subsidence: when soil expands and presses upwards against foundations and moves them. This normally only happens on clay subsoils.

Hip The sloping edge of the hipped plane of a roof.

Hip Iron Metal hook set at the base of hip tiles to support them.

Hip/Hip Rafter The external junction between roof slopes and the diagonally placed rafter forming this.

Hogging Mode Refers to the pattern of heave cracks, which are usually wider at the bottom that the top (opposite to sagging mode).

Hopper Head Funnel-type box at the top of a downpipe into which gutter pipes discharge.

Humane Trap Plastic see-through box, designed to lure a rodent inside and imprison it, so you can release it into the wild.

Humping/Kick Roof fault where the ridge drops at each end, rising in the middle.

Hylotrupes bajulus The longhorn beetle or the Camberley longhorn.

Hypha Strand of fungus that projects beyond an outbreak of rot, typically stretching across a wall.

Immersion Heater Electric heating element inside a domestic hot water cylinder, looking and working in a similar way to that of an electric kettle.

Inspection Chamber Box-like structure below ground outside the house that allows access to the main sewer pipe, with a removable metal lid, called a manhole cover. Modern ones are of plastic and come as a complete structure, older chambers are of brick.

Interlocking Tiles Tiles with edges that interlock against one another to achieve a weathertight seal.

Interstitial Condensation Condensation that is trapped within a structure, usually after rising up through a permeable surface. Potentially extremely harmful.

Joist Hanger Sturdy metal bracket designed to support the end of a timber joist, with a projecting tongue that is set into a mortar course in a wall, used to 'hang' a timber joist against a wall so that the timber doesn't touch the masonry, from where it can absorb dampness.

Joists Beams running along the loft's floor, forming the topside of the ceiling below, and sometimes linking principal rafters.

Juice Electricity/live current.

Kango Electric demolition hammer, for smashing concrete or removing rendering or demolishing brickwork.

Laced Valley Method of covering two tiled roof planes that meet at a valley by arranging tile-and-a-half widths diagonally.

Letter of Agreement Similar to the building contract, but a less formal document.

Listed Building One that has been officially recognized as being of architectural or historic importance.

Listed Building Consent Permission granted by the local authority to do work on a listed building.

Listings Mortar fillets that fill the joint between a roof covering and a wall or chimney.

Margin The area of a slate or tile that is exposed.

Mathematical Tiles Aka brick tiles, rebate tiles or weather tiles, made to cover a wall so as to imitate bricks.

Mayonnaise Colloquial name for a thick-bodied insecticide paste applied to timber, used for killing wood-boring beetles.

Moisture Meter Hand-held electronic device used to measure a wall's moisture content by assessing its electrical conductivity. In certain circumstances it can give unreliable results.

Nail Fatigue/Sickness Rusting of the old wire nails used to attach tiles or slates, allowing these to slip and/or fall.

Olive Small copper collar used in compression joints, fitted over the circumference of the pipe near its end, facilitating its compression by a surrounding nut, to create a watertight joint.

Parapet Uppermost row of stones projecting either side of a parapet wall above a flat roof.

Planning Permission This is granted by the local authority and serves to make sure that proposed new buildings or extensions or changes to existing ones don't adversely affect the character of the area.

Principal Rafters The main rafters that meet at an angle at the roof's apex and carry the rest of the roof plus its covering.

Principle Stopcock/Stopvalve The company's valve, usually accessible below a metal or plastic lid in the front garden, drive or pavement that can be turned on and off using a special long key.

PUPS Trade acronym for 'previously underpinned properties'.

Purlins Timbers running laterally across the roof, fixed to principal rafters (and supporting common rafters when these are installed).

Quoins Precisely cut stones that decorate the corners of a building.

Quotation Builder's fixed price for a job.

Rafters Beams that carry the battens or laths from which tiles or slates are hung.

Randoms Slates of random width, between 300 – 600mm (12 – 24in) in length.

Rattus norvegicus Britain's most common rodent, the brown rat.

Ridge Board Beam running along the roof's apex.

Ridge Tile Half-round or right-angled tile that sits on the roof's ridge, bridging the tiles on both planes, used for weatherproofing a ridge, including half-round, angled, decorative and hog's back styles.

Rising Main The main water pipe that goes from the point of entry in the house to the upstairs floors.

Rolling Contract Where your contract is only valid for one group of tasks at a time, and only carried over to the next if you are satisfied.

RSJ Acronym for Rolled Steel Joist, this is a heavy metal beam used when part of a wall is removed, for instance when two rooms have a dividing wall taken away. It is inserted with a specific length built within the wall at each end, and designed to carry a structural weight above that would otherwise be unsupported.

S*** Steel Scatalogical reference meaning inferior steel with a very high carbon content, subject to cracking easily, with no inherent strength.

Sagging Mode Refers to the pattern of diagonal tapering subsidence cracks with the widest edge at the top (opposite to hogging mode).

Sagging/Sag Roof fault where rafters bend along their length, causing slumps.

Sarking Felt/Felt Underlay Waterproof membrane fixed underneath battens, to act as a barrier against wind, snow and rain.

Sarking/Sarking Boards Timber planks nailed to rafters, forming a base for tiles or slates.

Scantle Roof Type of traditional slate roof, whereby the visible area of slate diminishes progressively towards the ridge.

Scratch Coat The first coat of render applied to a wall, scored to achieve maximum adhesion.

Serpula lacrymans The fungus dry rot.

Service Pipe Underground pipe leading from the principle stopvalve to your property.

Settlement The normal downwards compressive movement of a building into the ground as a result of its own weight; this is usually applicable to new constructions or extensions, and is normally slight and typically ends after about a year.

Shaling, Shattering De-laminating of a tile, usually as a result of frost damage.

Sharp Sand/Thames Washed Washed sand, used for flooring screeds and external rendering. Sharp and cutting when you squeeze it in your hand.

Site Meetings Periodic discussions between client and builder to assess progress and resolve problems.

Snagging List List of problems found after the completion of a project that need to be fixed.

Snaggings The niggling 'unfinished' jobs sometimes discovered at the end of a large job, that need to be discovered and attended to.

Soakaway Underground arrangement of bricks or blocks into which gutter water is channelled for dispersal into the subsoil. Modern building regulations stipulate that these should be a minimum distance from the house and have sufficient capability, but years ago a soakaway might simply be a pile of empty paint tins tossed into a hole, quite close to the house. These inevitably become blocked, in which case the water will disperse close to or on the building, possibly into the foundations.

Soakers Lead pieces used to weatherproof the junction between slates and an adjacent wall.

Soffit The timber panel underneath the roof's overhang at the eaves.

Soft Sand/Building Sand Unwashed sand. Used for bricklaying and pointing. Contains a certain amount of loam, or clay, and feels comfortably soft when squeezed in your hand.

Sole Plate Solid chunk of timber inserted between rafter and the wall's top.

Spalling The splitting and cracking of stonework, typically caused by the expansion of rusting ironwork contained within it.

Sparks Electrician.

Specification Expanded version of the brief, with a detailed breakdown of every aspect of the work, each section priced. Usually produced by a surveyor, architect or architectural technologist.

Spreading Roof fault where rafters splay outwards, sometimes pushing walls outwards too.

Stopcock/Valve Control tap for turning off water within the home.

Strongboy Supportive steel device with an arm stuck out at 90 degrees for supporting a structure from the side.

Strut Beams used either to hold structural timbers apart, or to link purlins to internal party walls, for enhanced support.

Stucco A form of decorative render, popular in Georgian times.

Subsidence Downward movement of a building's foundations caused by loss of support.

Surface Condensation When warm humid air precipitates moisture on a cold surface.

Swept Valley Method of covering two tiled or slated roof planes that meet at a valley, using specially shaped slates.

Tanking The process of providing a continuous impervious membrane over walls and floors in order to resist hydrostatic pressure.

Tender A bid from a builder to do some work.

Thermostatic Radiator Valve (TRV) Valve fitted to an individual radiator so that it blocks hot water's entry at a preset adjustable temperature.

Throat Part of a flue above the fire.

Tie Beams Horizontal timber ties linking the bases of two principal rafters.

Tile-and-a-Half Slate or tile that is one-and-a-half times the standard width, used at verges in alternate rows to facilitate staggered gaps.

Tilting Batten Thicker batten, used near the ridge, to tilt up the top edges of tiles or slates.

Tilting Fillet Wedge-shaped batten used to tilt the side edges of a row of tiles or slates.

Tingle Flat metal hook, used to support individual repair slates.

Torching The traditional method of applying a layer of mortar on part of the underside of tiles or slates which still allows roof to 'breathe'.

Trickle Vent Slot-shaped vent in a wall near double-glazed windows to counteract their air-insulating qualities.

True Dry Rot   The historic name for dry rot.

Truss   Triangular or A-shaped unit supporting purlins, sometimes joined by a tie beam or collar.

Truss Frame   Framework of timbers forming a section of a roof structure.

Undercloak   Double course of slates or tiles at the eaves or verges.

Underpinning   A method of replacing or reinforcing the ground beneath foundations to provide support.

Upstand   The section of roofing felt that extends above the roofing area, folded upwards, to be built into between courses of a low parapet wall so water cannot penetrate at the roof's edges.

Valley   Internal junction between roof slopes.

Valley Gutter   Normally of lead, and positioned at the base of a valley.

Vapour Control Layer   Sheet of waterproof material (bitumen felt or metal foil-covered felt) typically used beneath the insulation on a 'warm roof' method of flat roof construction, so as to prevent moisture entering the roof void.

Verge   Open edge (side) of roof.

Vertical Tiles   Tiles with a shallow camber, designed to be fixed onto walls rather than roofs.

Wall Plate   Beam laid along the top of a wall, to which rafters are fixed.

Weil's Disease   Serious illness that can be caught from contact with rat's urine.

Windy (Tools)   Those that run using compressed air.

Xestobium rufovillosum   Deathwatch beetle (DWB).

Contacts

SPECIALISTS

Bar Preservation (www.barpreservation.co.uk; 0161 655 3480) (Manchester). This is a structural repair and preservation specialist offering to undertake bespoke repairs and installations in all types of construction. Expertise in damp-proofing, timber preservation and structural repairs (cavity wall-tie problems, subsidence, etc.) since 1989 (also basement waterproofing and conversion).

Brian Clancy, Brian Clancy Higby Partnership (www.brianclancyhigby.co.uk; 01565 7577 90) (Knutsford, Cheshire). Specialist structural engineers.

Coopers Chartered Consulting Engineers (www.coopers.co.uk; 01244 684910) (Chester). A thriving and innovative independent consultancy, a family-run business. They have been providing expertise in civil, structural, geotechnical and environmental engineering since 1982.

Denis Townend (01737 814120) (Epsom). Consultant structural engineer, wide range of experience.

Hutton + Rostron Environmental Investigations Ltd (www.handr.co.uk; 01483 203221) (Gomshall, Surrey). Phone for details of northern branch.

Ingram Consultancy Ltd (www.ingram-consultancy.co.uk; 01749 850900) (Upton Noble, Somerset). Surveyors' practice, specializing in historic buildings.

Joanna Haydon Knowell, JHK Estate Agency, residential lettings and management (www.jhk.co.uk; 020 8883 5485) (North London).

Julian Owen, architect (www.julianowen.co.uk; 0115 922 9831) (Nottingham). Julian has a vast range of experience with numerous domestic and commercial projects, extensions, alterations, conversions including the complete restoration of historic buildings. He is also a prolific author (see Chapter 1).

KMASS Consulting Structural and Civil engineers (www.kmass.co.uk; 01727 875571 and 020 3384 6848) (St. Albans and London). This structural engineering practice was founded in 2000 in response to the demands of its clients and has developed to include a range of building design, structural design, civil and engineering services throughout London and the south-east.

Peter Cox (www.petercox.com; 0808 149 2336 or 0845 222 0404). Peter Cox, not an individual but a large company, specializes in damp control, woodworm, dry rot and wet rot, cavity wall-tie repair and basement waterproofing and has branches throughout the UK.

Ridout Associates (www.ridoutassociates.co.uk; 01562 885135) (Stourbridge, East Midlands). Team of independent consultants who specialize in the scientific assessment of timber decay and other damp-related problems.

Robert Demaus, Demaus Building Diagnostics (01568 615662) (Leominster). Robert Demaus is an expert in building investigations using pioneering techniques.

Roger Mears, Conservation Architects (www. rmears.co.uk; 020 7359 8222) (North London). Roger's practice was founded in 1980 and he has built up a reputation for sensitive work to a vast number of historic and domestic buildings.

Roy Ilott & Associates (www.royilottsurveyors. co.uk; 01372 727926 and 01985 211152) (Epsom, Surrey and Warminster). Consultant chartered building surveyors. Roy Ilott FRICS, has a wide experience in building maintenance and repairs over more than forty years. He now specializes in building defect analysis, dilapidations on commercial and rented residential properties and party wall issues. He provides reports for various problems based on this experience, and I am grateful for his assistance when requested.

Subsidence Claims Advisory Bureau (SCAB) and sister company Bureau Insurance Services (www. subsidencebureau.com; 0845 3006127). Proprietor Robert Hooker is an insurance specialist.

Target Fixings Ltd (www.targetfixings.com; 01488 686311) (Hungerford, Berkshire). This company have been designing and installing solutions for over fifteen years offering stabilization to properties affected by moisture, wall-tie failure, bowing walls, delamination, etc., and also manufacture the tooling and cementitious grout for their fixings. They produce the Target Heli Pile system, a versatile, quick and simple solution to many foundation-related problems, including those caused by subsidence and heave. Aluminium Heli Piles are used in combination with the Bar Flex Beaming system, a 'pile-and-beam' repair method.

Warren Woodworm and Waverley Building Preservation (www.warrenwoodworm.co.uk; 01428 606786) (Farnham, Surrey). Specialists in extermination of wood-boring insects, eradication of wood decay and control of rising and penetrating damp and condensation.

ORGANIZATIONS AND COMPANIES that have not already been mentioned in previous pages, or their details not given.

Anglia Lime Company (www.anglialime.com; 01787 313974) (Sudbury, Suffolk). Supply lime putty and natural hydraulic limes, readymix mortars and palters, mortar matching service, technical advice.

Association of British Insurers, ABI (www.abi.org. uk; 020 7600 3333).

Association of Specialist Underpinning Contractors (ASUCplus) (www.asuc.org.uk; 01252 739143).

British Insurance Brokers' Association (BIBA) (www.biba.org.uk; 'Find a broker helpline' 0870 950 1790).

Docherty Chimney Group (www.docherty.co.uk; 01635 292400). Quality chimney products.

Floodtite Systems, Home Flood Protection (www. floodtite.com; 020 8442 0872) (North London). Suppliers of Kitemarked flood barriers, door panels, airbrick covers and other devices for floodproofing your home.

John Moore Specialist Resins (07973 118476). Professional exterior coatings for buildings.

Klargester (www.klargester.com; 01296 633000) (Aylesbury, Bucks). The UK's market leading brand in off-mains drainage systems, part of Kingspan Environmental. Sewage treatment plants, etc.

RJW Associates (www.rjw-associates.co.uk; 020 8393 7954). Financial advice on mortgages, loans and insurance.

Strippers Paint Removers (www.stripperspaintremovers.com; 01787 371524). Mail order service for paint stripping products, technical advice re stripping paint from all kinds of surface.

Zurich Insurance (www.zurich.co.uk).

Index